JULIA McGUINNESS is a cou... ... ...yer
Briggs consultant at Creative ... ...
is also a member of Lapidus, ...
the practice and teaching of ... ...riting, and the ...
of *Growing Spiritually with the Myers-B...*

'McGuinness explains, better than anyone I have read, the 16
personality types in Myers-Briggs, and then goes on to explore
further subtleties in each type. She strikes a good balance between
commending each person's "best-fit" type, and celebrating the
"endless range of unique individuals".'

Christianity

'[The author's] gifts bring readers a sophisticated understanding
of the interplay between this psychological approach and Christian
faith ...'

Church Times

WRITING OUR FAITH

JULIA McGUINNESS

First published in Great Britain in 2013

Society for Promoting Christian Knowledge
36 Causton Street
London SW1P 4ST
www.spckpublishing.co.uk

British Library Cataloguing-in-Publication Data
A catalogue record for this book is available from the British Library

ISBN 978–0–281–06963–7
eBook ISBN 978–0–281–06964–4

Typeset by Graphicraft Limited, Hong Kong
First printed in Great Britain by Ashford Colour Press
Subsequently digitally printed in Great Britain

eBook by Graphicraft Limited, Hong Kong

Produced on paper from sustainable forests

Contents

Preface

This book brings together different genres and approaches to writing – therapeutic, devotional, expressive and creative – within the context of Christian faith. I would like to thank those who have generously supported me with their time and input. Some have shared their writing experiences; others have tried particular exercises and fed back on them for me. Their stories are a vital part of this book. Family and friends have given time in another sense – tolerating my absence as I have disappeared into my study or gone to the hospitable silence of Gladstone's Library in Hawarden, to work on the book yet again. For all these, I am very grateful.

Julia McGuinness

1

Writing and the Word

———◆●◆———

I walked in silence, save for my shoes' steady crunch on the marked gravel pathway. The breeze rustled through the nearby trees, but I didn't look up. My attention was fixed on the twisting course of the labyrinth path beneath my feet.

I'd snatched a few days for an autumn retreat at St Beuno's Ignatian Retreat Centre in North Wales. I felt fragmented, aware of demands pulling me in all directions. Before setting out to prayer-walk the labyrinth in the grounds, I picked up my pen and opened my journal. I wrote down the things that were on my mind. I wrote my prayers – that morning, just a list of questions I had for God, starting with 'How should I spend my time?' Then I closed the book and went outdoors to listen for God.

Unsure how to pray as I paced the labyrinth, I decided simply to give thanks for all the disparate bits of my life past and present, exactly as they were – including, as I noted later, 'the rubbish stuff'.

At the labyrinth's centre-point was a disc of rock marked with the Greek alphabet letters of Jesus' title – *Alpha* and *Omega*. It felt a bit presumptuous to step onto it, but I did. Afterwards I wrote: 'Felt I needed to stand there longer than comfortable. Long enough to watch individual leaves fall; the clouds move; the long twigs rustle against the skyline, long enough to feel grounded.' I walked out with a sense of peace and a feeling that something had shifted.

As I journalled this experience later, I began to gain a sense of what it was. Nothing outwardly was different, yet my life's different strands from English teacher to therapeutic counsellor, alongside an ongoing love of all forms of writing, especially for personal growth and spiritual journeying, all seemed to link up.

It was a turning point. Ever since, I've sought to foster these connections: to bring writing into counselling practice; to make the most of personal writing's potential – devotional, therapeutic and creative – and encourage others to do the same. This book is part of that journey out from the labyrinth's centre.

The privilege and power of writing

I've known Claire for years – we met as undergraduates study-ing English together. But it was only recently I learned why she became a primary school teacher and now, as an English specialist tutor on a PGCE course, prepares others for the same profession.

> One summer, when I was still a student, I was standing in the queue at the post office. I saw someone who couldn't read or write really struggling at the counter. She asked me to read her letter for her, because she couldn't. I realized what an advantage I had in being literate. If I could teach children these skills, it could make a huge difference to their lives.

Claire was right. Literacy is an essential toolkit for survival in today's society, enabling us to participate fully in our community and access all we need. Most of us take it for granted. We pick up a book and start reading, pick up a pen or open up a laptop keyboard and start writing. We write for ourselves, for others at work and home, to those we know well or for those we have never met personally.

At its most straightforward level, writing something down for ourselves can:

- remind us of things we need to do;
- capture a moment we want to remember;
- order and prioritize our tasks;
- make sense of a problem we want to work out;
- express our creativity.

But writing is more than a basic skill. We can write to others to communicate information, but we can also use the written word to deepen personal relationships, whether through letters, cards or emails. Putting the things we appreciate about another into written form, for example, gives us space to think about what we *really* want to say. It creates something permanent, which can be treasured for a lifetime. It could also help us broach a difficult subject, paving the way for a conversation to follow.

Writing for ourselves can also be much more than our factual memory's safety net. The power of writing for well-being and healing has received increasing attention in recent years. Significant pioneering research was started in the 1980s by Dr James Pennebaker, Professor in the Psychology Department at the University of Austin at Texas.

Dr Pennebaker's research involved asking participants to explore their thoughts and feelings about a current emotional upheaval in a daily 15-minute period of continuous writing over three to five consecutive days. Outcomes were compared with those of a control group instructed to write factually about neutral topics, such as the day's activities.

The results revealed that although some emotionally expressive writers felt some immediate discomfort and distress in the writing task in the short term, they experienced measurable benefits to their longer-term physical health: lower blood pressure, better sleeping patterns, stronger immune systems, raised mood, improved working memory and fewer visits to the doctor.[1]

We all know how stress or grief can make us physically ill. As Dr Pennebaker observes, emotional upheaval affects 'all aspects of who we are – our financial situation, our relationships with others, our view of ourselves, our issues of life and death'. Being able to disclose whatever is troubling us is a first step towards resolving the issue. 'Writing,' says Dr Pennebaker, 'helps us focus and organize the experience.'

Where we cannot speak out our concerns to an empathic listener for whatever reason, the blank page or screen is always receptive. We may even prefer to start by writing rather than talking. Expressing our thoughts and feelings in the written word helps us attend to them, embodying them in a separate form that we can actually see. We may still have the issue, but brought to light it somehow no longer has us. We have some substance to work with, so we can address the matter more fruitfully.

At a deeper level, writing something down can help us:

- express in a safe space what might be hard to say elsewhere;
- release the pressure of unspoken feelings so we can let go;
- shape and contain overwhelming thoughts and feelings;
- identify an issue more clearly;
- reveal insights we did not consciously know were there;
- rehearse and prepare for upcoming situations that cause us anxiety;
- have a record to add to, reflect on or reshape.

As writing's contribution to well-being is increasingly validated by researchers and encouraged by therapists, we might naturally turn to the part it could play in our Christian lives on our journey towards wholeness in body, mind *and* spirit. Writing may foster a deeper connection with others and ourselves, but how does it relate to growing our communion with God? Can we write our faith? Christine's experience suggests we can:

> When I first came to England from the States, aged 18, I went to college to study art. I married a year later, and became a mother the year after that. Motherhood so young and far away from 'home' was quite tough. When we later moved away from the friends I'd made those first few years and the supportive church we were in, I felt isolated and alone. Writing became who I talked to and reading was who I listened to. I do not think my faith would have stayed so grounded otherwise.
>
> Writing down what I was thinking and feeling was, in a very real sense, praying. I find it hard to focus on prayer in other ways – my mind goes off in various directions, easily distracted. Writing helped me focus on and untangle things, and I addressed what I wrote to my Lord. Most was simple prose, but some became poetry. The extra challenge of finding the right word for the right place helped me take my writing beyond just whingeing into something more powerful and healing.

From living Word to written word

Perhaps we can expect the written word to make a difference, as the Christian faith is centred on words that bring life and, most supremely, the living Word himself.

The Bible opens with God using words to speak Creation into being in the book of Genesis. The redemptive power of words inhabits the New Testament, through Jesus' words. John's Gospel presents Jesus as God's Word, come to live among us (John 1.14) and make the mystery of God's nature visible. We are invited to 'read' Jesus, God's living Word, and respond to his call to salvation and wholeness in God's kingdom.

God's written word includes a range of writing genres: laws in Leviticus; historical records in Kings and Chronicles; epigrammatic wisdom in Proverbs; the psalmist's expressive outpourings of prayer; Gospel biographies of the incarnate Jesus; Apostles' letters to instruct, correct and encourage; the image-rich, allusive language of prophecy from Ezekiel to Revelation.

The Christian Church has long treasured literacy. After the Roman Empire's decline, monasteries arose as centres of education and scholarship across Europe, housing libraries and scriptoria – literally 'places for writing' – where manuscripts were copied. Bede and the monks who authored the Anglo-Saxon Chronicle were early writers of our nation's history.

Christians such as Robert Raikes were forerunners of the State's introduction of weekday schooling in 1870. He started a Sunday School in Gloucester in 1780, to prevent local slum children from falling into crime – Sunday was the only day that poor, factory-working children could attend. Raikes used the Bible as a textbook to teach them to read and write. By 1784, John Wesley's journal records that Sunday School classes were 'springing up everywhere'. By 1831, there were 1.2 million children in Sunday Schools – about 25 per cent of the population.[2]

Down the ages, Christians' responses to Scripture and the Spirit have generated a proliferation of written words. Teaching has been a cornerstone, from the Desert Fathers' wisdom to biblical commentaries; St Ignatius' 'Spiritual Exercises' to Rick Warren's *The*

Purpose-driven Life. We may have read published Christian literature in many genres: letters and journals; plays and poetry; testimony and fiction. But words in print are nowhere near the sum total of private Christian writing seen by no one other than God and perhaps a few trusted friends.

Personally writing our faith

Personal writing, whether published or not, can help us hold our course, as well as encourage others, on our journey of Christian faith. It is primarily this sort of writing that we are exploring in this book.

As well as formal Bible study or note-taking, our personal Christian writing may:

- record things God has done in our lives so we do not forget;
- chart our personal faith journey in its ups and downs;
- reflect on an issue to understand or explore it more deeply;
- list or write our prayers;
- express our emotions about God or to him;
- prepare for a particular meeting or conversation;
- explore our hopes and desires;
- gain insight into the heart of a problem;
- confess and repent;
- create something beautiful for God.

I have a notebook with me all of the time. In fact, I've got lots of notebooks all over the place! My mind is constantly thinking about things. I'll jot down prayers, a sentence, some Scripture, or even just a couple of words.

I've always kept personal journals. Writing helps me to make sense of things and also empty myself of things. I grew up in circumstances where offloading was not allowed. I was not allowed to speak and did not have a place of my own to think. My mind was constantly full of things I wanted to say, but couldn't.

Writing really helps me get stuff out of the way. If I let things build up, I end up very depressed. It's a strategy to blurb everything out, put it outside myself, and then throw it away. It's a way of release.

Carolyn

Think about what writing means to you. Do you turn to words when you are sad or troubled, happy or when something important is happening, such as a special holiday or anniversary? Do you like your writing to take you on flights of fancy or are you more comfortable with the facts and describing what is around you? Do you write to make sense of a muddle and understand an issue, or to pour out powerful feelings, restore calm and bring perspective?

It does not matter if you have not previously made a faith and writing connection. Even professional writers do not all come into their own at the same stage. Paul Torday, whose first book, *Salmon Fishing in the Yemen*, was published when he was aged 59, observed in a BBC Radio 4 *Open Book* programme that the energy for writing may rise up at different seasons of a writer's life. It may be the same on our Christian journey.

An unexpected period of illness or loss may draw people towards the written word, perhaps to record and reflect on what is happening or provide an outlet for expressing feelings when they are alone or unable to be fully active. Some survivors of traumatic experiences use writing to bear witness to what they have been through.

Brian Keenan's book, *An Evil Cradling*, recounts his four-and-a-half years as a hostage in Beirut. In the preface he describes writing it as 'part of a long process of healing', a process he sees as 'self-exploratory and therapeutic'. The book is based on facts and experiences, but Keenan is also aware that piecing together his memories to seek the sense and meaning in his story gives his book a 'reflective and meditative' quality. Writing both what happened and his response has contributed to his healing.

Writing during a period of upheaval in life may also help affirm our worth, orientate ourselves and keep us going. Some people find that after the storm is over, they want to incorporate more personal writing into their lives, to help them live at a richer, more reflective pace.

Christians may use writing as a discipline for a particular issue or season. Rachel D. Hackenberg, author of *Writing to God: 40 Days of Praying with My Pen*,[3] challenged herself to 'add a daily rhythm' to her erratic prayer-writing practice, by writing a prayer every day throughout Lent.

Our personalities may also affect our relationship to personal writing. Introverted personalities, who prefer to replenish their energies through time in their inner world, are likely to turn more naturally to writing. They can write alone, in private space and quiet, uninterrupted rather than pressed into interaction. For such personalities, placing words on a page can be a safe way of making them visible in the outer world. From there, they may move out to share selected writings with others.

Those with more extraverted personalities may prefer to process issues by talking things out rather than thinking them through, verbalizing their thoughts and feelings. Yet such outgoing personalities can find writing valuable, a helpful counter-balance in helping them slow to a more reflective pace, get closer to their inner life, and stay focused on what is most important. The physical act of writing also meets their desire to do something active, rather than just observe passively.

Whether our lives are busy or our minds are buzzing, the act of writing can slow us down. Transposing our inner thoughts and feelings to marks on a page involves both mental and physical concentration. This helps us focus more intently. We have to hold the pen and control its movements to shape and order the words. Even pressing a computer keyboard connects us more fully to the process.

A couple of concerns

It's an all too common experience for those who want to write. As we finally sit down and pick up our pen, two 'characters' turn up to put a dampener on the enterprise: the Inner Critic and the Inner Censor. Our Inner Censor prohibits what words we may want to put on the page, and if we do manage to write, our Inner Critic is sure to tell us that it's not good enough. The danger is that we will never risk writing anything, for fear of it being sub-standard or wrong.

How confident are you about your writing ability? Are you fully to grips with grammar or do you struggle with spelling?

Inner Critics are sticklers for correctness, but their services are not required here. This writing is more a personal *process* than a published product. Considerations such as spelling, punctuation and grammar only come into play if you wish to publicize your writing more widely, when clear shaping and technical accuracy will make it more accessible.

If writing is a process, the same goes for our Christian life. We are redeemed but still imperfect, and in the process of being made whole. We may want to write about the doubts, fears, anger or unforgivenness that reflect our frailty rather than our faith. If we desire to use personal writing to draw closer to God, the Inner Censor, even in its theological guise, cannot prohibit us from bringing these areas into the open space of God's love that the page can represent. Being able to start from where we are is part of what enables us to grow.

Some may worry that personal writing could become self-indulgent. Helen Cepero, writing on Christian journalling, notes that like 'all spiritual disciplines and practices', this writing is about 'learning to be aware and awake, open to God, ourselves and the world around us'.[4]

When the psalmist writes, 'Search me, O God, and know my heart; test me and know my thoughts' (Psalm 139.23), the object is not a dead-end introspection but a drawing out of what is within, so that he might be led 'in the way everlasting'. Exposure on the page can become a stepping stone towards resolving an area that needs healing, forgiveness and renewal. This was so for Linda.

Linda thinks it was the smell of coffee that triggered the memory. After all, it was after the writing workshop's mid-morning break at the church centre's coffee bar that I asked the group to write a conversation between themselves today and their younger self, at whatever age and stage they wished.

Linda found herself recalling the day she first tasted coffee as a little girl. She remembered how the adults, gathered at her grandparents' house, had seemed especially kind that day, as she loaded spoonfuls of sugar into her cup without being told off.

Linda's father died in hospital, around the time of her fifth birthday, but she was never directly told of his death. Her mother had already left the marriage for the man who soon became Linda's stepfather. During her childhood, where there was tension between her mother and stepfather, Linda felt the strain – and the blame. Writing to herself as a young child brought up some sensitivities that had never really left her.

Linda told me some weeks later that writing about this incident had stayed in her mind. 'The next night I couldn't sleep', she said. 'I found myself wondering why the adults were all so nice to me that day. Was that my birthday, or was it when they knew my father had just died?'

Linda reflected and prayed about this memory. Her writing had reconnected her with what it felt like to be that small child, vulnerable and powerless. Her prayers began to help her see this child-self through more Christlike, compassionate eyes. 'I think it's helped me come to terms with things, and be a bit kinder to myself', she told me. Linda's past had not changed, but by letting go of some guilt and self-judgement, her relationship to it did.

Linda was surprised at what emerged when she picked up her pen. Perhaps this makes us wonder what will surface if we start writing more deeply. Will we be overwhelmed with painful personal material?

Our writing may draw out things buried beneath our everyday awareness, but we can trust the process. As Gillie Bolton, consultant in therapeutic writing, notes, 'writing is a kind and comparatively gentle way of facing whatever there is to be faced'.[5] She observes that what she calls your 'trustworthy self' will enable you to 'write material you can learn from but not allow you to write things that you would find unbearable to read or relate to', even if what does emerge causes some discomfort on the way, as it did for Linda.

As Christians, we can be assured that our trustworthy God – all-loving, all-knowing and all-wise – watches over our writing process. Whatever the Holy Spirit allows to surface is no surprise to him. He is releasing it into our consciousness at this time for his good purposes. So you can approach writing without fear, even if with a little uncertainty.

You may wish to share your writing with someone you trust if you need support in working through an issue it has highlighted, or even link up with a writing friend from the start, for some mutual encouragement.

Encouragement from others can also quieten our Inner Critic. This may especially help if you write primarily to explore the potential, power and pattern of words, and enjoy expressing your God-given creativity.

There is no one-size-fits-all prescription for writing in the context of your faith. It is your personal response to God, whether your writing emphasis is expressive, creative or devotional. Some types of writing may appeal more than others. Sometimes pressing on in a writing task beyond what you think you can do releases rich and unexpected material; at other times, it is better not to force the issue. So use this book's suggestions at whatever level is appropriate for you. Explore widely, write deeply, and enjoy practising your more favoured approaches as you integrate writing into your faith journey.

Some things to try

1 Write about writing

Write about your own writing, reviewing how you have used it to date. You could use the following sentence openings as prompts, finishing the sentence writing a longer paragraph if you wish:

- This last week, I have written . . . (You could simply list the different sorts of writing you have done – which may include a list!)
- For me, writing at school was . . .
- The sort of writing I prefer to do is . . . because . . .
- If I knew I could write anything at all, it would be . . . because . . .
- What helps me write is . . .
- What gets in the way of my writing is . . .
- The way I feel about writing and faith is . . .

Read and reflect on what you have written. You may wish to thank God for the ability to write, or pray about any barriers to your writing that you have identified – lack of time, concerns about privacy or 'correctness', self-criticism and so on.

2 Turning point

My labyrinth-walk at St Beuno's marked a personal turning point. Writing down my questions to God helped me name and put aside my concerns. Writing my thoughts and feelings after the prayer-walk brought other insights to the surface. It clarified what I sensed God was saying, and helped me understand it better by putting it into words I could see. Once I had grasped this new focus, I could work with it and let it inform my decisions.

Write about a personal turning point in your own life, noting:

- your feelings and outlook prior to that point;
- what brought about the change, whether in situation or attitude;
- what the change was and how life became different from that point.

As you write and reread your writing, do you see more in your story than you realized was there at the time?

If you are seeking a turning point at the moment, write down your concerns and questions to God. Leave this writing for a week, during which you seek to be open and receptive to however God may want to speak or act in your life. After this period, reread your questions and concerns. Write about how things are now. If nothing seems different, write about that as a prayer giving things over to God again, trusting his timing in changing you or your situation.

2

Journalling and getting started

Anne pulls a clutch of hardback books with colourful covers out of the canvas bag beside her chair. She has come to chat with me about her journalling. We sit in a snug conservatory, cat asleep on a nearby chair, spring rain falling softly on the garden outside.

Some journals look well worn and clearly go back a long way. Anne starts idly flicking through them. From where I sit, I can see large, rounded handwriting ranging across and around the blank pages. Anne seems to forget me, absorbed by what she's reading. 'I didn't realize I started writing poetry so early', she murmurs.

Anne wrote a journal as a teenager, but then stopped for around 12 years before starting to journal 'properly' again in 2007. Some books are only half full, as she abandoned them for new starts with new volumes, like the time she decided to make her journal a very specific record of her prayer-life.

Anne says she does not journal every day:

I tend to write when I'm really stressed about something, and I've exhausted avenues of spoken reasoning. Then there are the things I can't or don't want to talk about with other people – maybe intimate things to do with my marriage. There aren't many people in church you can talk to about these things. I also wrote when I was having real problems at work, and everyone was sick of me talking about it. There are only so many people you can talk to about something without just ending up repeating yourself.

As we start to write our faith, we need to think about where we will write it. We may want to gather our writing in a Christian journal if we want to keep it as a resource to reread, rework or refer to. In this chapter we will look at aspects of setting up a faith journal and explore some types of writing we might do within it.

Christian journalling has a long history. We may have been inspired and encouraged by the published journals of prominent Christian figures such as John Wesley, William Wilberforce and Henri Nouwen, but these are only a few among the many Christians who have found the practice of journalling helpful in charting the course of their ordinary Christian lives.

Perhaps, like me, you remember being given a five-year diary as a childhood Christmas present, complete with tiny metal lock and key. I remember how my New Year enthusiasm for this half-decade project was flagging by March. By the school summer holidays, my diary entries had run dry. I thought about trying again next time around, but it felt like cheating to go on to Year 2 when I'd fallen at the fence of Year 1.

Fortunately, a faith journal is not like a diary to be kept religiously day in, day out. The word journal derives from the French 'jour' for day, but it also relates to 'journee', a word that covers *what can be done* in a day-long period – work accomplished or distance travelled. We may use our journal to explore things done or stages on our Christian journey, rather than as a daily account of activities per se.

My own journals are hardbacked, widelined books – usually plain black – in which I date entries as I go. Sometimes my journal writing has been irregular and brief. At others, particularly when I have a lot going on in life, it has been much more profuse. On retreat, where I have more time to listen and write, it is an essential.

Writing a Christian journal brings a rhythm to my day. It's good to externalize things, even though seeing what I've written in honesty can be painful. Seeing my words written down can change the way I think about something as I reflect on it.

Writing slows me down so my thoughts and prayers come through. It lets the creative side come to the fore. It's also helpful to record good and bad times. Rereading these later can bring encouragement and hope, especially if I've tried to capture what I sense God has been saying to me. *Pat*

It can be helpful to journal through a significant season: to counteract pre-Christmas busyness in Advent; write your prayers in Lent; capture the unique journey of a pilgrimage or trip; work through a particular issue, perhaps a challenging time of loss or illness; to chart a change – house-move, new phase of life, pregnancy, retirement, starting out in a ministry and so on.

Writing a faith journal through changing times can help anchor you amid uncertainty and possible loneliness. You can explore questions, express feelings and note what you are learning. As we write through change, God may change us through writing. This may be especially so if our circumstances are forcing us to take life at a slower pace. I know some who have felt sustained by expressive journal writing through a life-changing illness, such as breast cancer. As Anne illustrates, a seasonal journal can be brought to an end, even if you have not filled every page in your book.

> I choose my journal carefully. I like blank pages. Lines can feel constricting. The paper needs to be of good quality and I write with a fountain pen. For me this reflects that attending to my innermost being is a precious thing.
>
> My journalling tends to be a bit spasmodic. I'm always needing to take the time to stop being too busy, and it helps even if I only write for ten minutes in a day. That's what keeps me attentive. When I don't do it, I miss things.
>
> In my head, the activity is in the same compartment as praying. *Ricarda*

There are many Christian journalling books on the market if you do not wish to create your own. These generally have lined pages, attractive covers of various designs and Bible quotations throughout. Some are notebooks, wire-bound to allow open pages to lie flat for easier writing. Others are leather-bound, with heavier, gilt-edged paper. As one satisfied customer commented, having a beautiful, designated book 'makes me feel like writing'. You could choose from:

- a special, high-quality hardback book to reflect the value of your writing;

- a loose-leaf notebook to help you write freely without feeling you have to write perfectly, and be able to tear pages out more easily;
- a large book to contain a lot of your writing in one location;
- a smaller book to carry around;
- an attractively produced Christian journal with Bible quotes;
- a non-specific book to date and section as you please;
- a lined book to keep your writing even;
- a blank book, so you can write in different directions, draw or doodle.

Traditionally, the Christian journal has been upheld as a place to record sermon and Bible study notes, quotes and prayer lists. Your journal may include writing to learn, but we can also be enriched by many other ways of writing our faith.

Writing practitioner Luann Budd says that Christian writing for spiritual growth need not always be a serious business: 'Many of us believe that being creative is really playing, so we don't give ourselves the freedom to be creative during our devotional times.' If we do, however, she asserts that our God-given creativity 'may lead us to write a short story, a drama, a poem or song.'[1]

A Christian journal could include:		
Descriptions	Lists and notes	Songs
Reflections	Flow-writing	Quotes
Questions	Letters	Stories
Dreams	Plans	Drama
Poems	Prayers	Mind-maps
What will you put in yours?		

Think, too, about how to organize your writing. Some like to separate different sorts of writing within one book, making it easier to track down something specific. Others prefer simply to date each new entry as they write, making it easier to see the day-by-day connections between different aspects.

I write by dated entries into one book, relying on memory and an idea of date to locate what I want to reread. You could colour-code types of writing in different inks, or number pages and create an index if you wanted to be more efficient.

An A4 file with dividers is more versatile, enabling you to mix, match and move around journal entries as you wish. Dr Ira Progoff, a psychotherapist who found that journal-writing clients tended to work through their issues more rapidly, developed an intensive journalling method in the 1960s. His workshop participants kept their writing in ring-binders, sectioned into different areas, including aspects such as personal relationships, health, dreams and meaning in life.

You may wish to use more than one book at a time – some people have several on the go. Jane uses one to record things she senses she has heard directly from God; another for reflective writing; a third where she writes letters to God. I think I would find this rather too fragmentary.

An increasingly popular option, particularly, it seems, with men, is journalling on to a computer screen. Various Christian journalling software programmes are available, although they carry the risk of becoming outdated.

The versatility of a tablet journal is part of its appeal for Ian: 'You can write in a tablet nearly anywhere and at any time', he tells me. Bible verses or other references can be easily imported into the text; screen background and writing font can be changed; it is secure and portable. Another advantage is being able to search for specific entries and topics by using keywords.

'Whenever my mother-in-law had filled a diary, she'd soak it in a bucket to dissolve the ink', said a fellow journal writer, as we discussed the issue of confidentiality, adding, 'I wouldn't like anyone to get hold of what I've written. It's so fearlessly honest.'

If we are going to use our journal to put words to things we have never dared express before – jealousy of a sister's success; resentment of a friend's demands; fears of illness; doubts of God's reality; struggles with an ageing parent – we need to be sure that our page is a safe space. Our writing may reflect a work in progress, an issue we want to explore in God's presence, but protected from others' eyes. Think about where to keep your journal, and ensure that those you live with respect its privacy. Computer files can be password-protected, and perhaps stored on a memory stick.

I asked Anne about how concerned she was about confidentiality: 'I was an only child, so I didn't have people prying', she said. 'And I trust my husband's integrity. He knows me so well anyway. I sometimes wonder what he'd think if he read what I've written about him. I guess we'd talk about it together.'

The next priority is setting aside time to write. Will it be morning, when you can write about your hopes for the day and dreams of the night? Or evening, with its opportunity to review the day past, catch its significant moments and reflect more deeply on events? Do you write better in longer blocks of time over the week, or in shorter daily snatches? Do you prefer to write at home or at another location, such as a library or café? Do you need silence or are you more comfortable with some background noise?

Putting words on the page

Later in this chapter we will explore four writing modes, to make us more aware of the range of writing approaches. But first we will look at the start- and end-point of the writing process. Genesis 1.1 reads, 'In the beginning when God created the heavens and the earth, the earth was a formless void and darkness covered the face of the deep.'

God's creation process brings separation – light from dark, sky from sea, water from land. He shapes the cosmos and evolves new elements – plants, trees, sun, moon and stars. Then comes the diversity of animal life – from birds, fish and other animals to humankind. As Genesis 2 opens, 'the heavens and the earth were finished, and all their multitude', and God rests, his creation complete.

This creative movement from formless substance to detailed shaping is reflected in the writing process. The observations, insights, thoughts and feelings inside our heads become articulated in visible shapes expressed on the page.

Of course, even when we have written words down, we may continue shaping them. We read over our writing, dismiss some sections and select others to develop; refine, reword and reorder our material. We may do a lot of this, especially if we want others to read what we have written; we may do very little or nothing. How much we do depends on the purpose of our writing. But at some point we will decide it is finished.

We can be inhibited from writing at all if we feel our writing has to arrive on the page in finished form. It doesn't – we can work on it when it is out there. It is better at first to get things down, rather than get them right, simply writing, noting and exploring, as free of any Inner Critic's intervention as we can be.

One way of helping to ignore our Inner Critic is to try some flow-writing. Sometimes known as free writing, speed writing or morning pages, flow-writing is a limbering up activity.

Exploring flow-writing

Write continuously for ten minutes, just putting on paper whatever comes to mind, without thinking or, most importantly, stopping. Ignore neatness and correctness. If you run out of things to write, just keep writing – even 'I have run out of things to write' – until you get going again.

Use one of the following suggestions as your opening words:

- This morning is . . .
- The way I see it . . .
- Sometimes . . .
- I wonder . . .

Flow-writing can help clear the decks of surface preoccupations, get us working with words and start to release our creativity. As you read back over what you have written, you may find personal concerns that you simply want to leave with God so that you can concentrate, free of worry. But you may also discover what the writer Virginia Woolf called 'diamonds in the dust heap' – a word or phrase that catches your particular attention. It may be an unusual word, striking phrase or surprising insight.

Circle or underline any potential 'diamonds' in the flow-writing you have just done.

Dorothy says she flow-writes daily as a prelude to personal Bible study:

> I write three pages of A5 first thing every morning. It gets rid of all my stresses, lets me know what's bothering me and raises questions. I see it as part of my devotions. I've never any idea what it's going to produce.

A flow-write can also help us warm up our writing muscles by putting words on the page. As the writer Julia Cameron notes in *The Right to Write*, 'Perfectionism is a primary writer's block.'[2] Flow-writing can give us permission to write our Christian faith as we are, where we are, not how we think we should be. It may also open doors to what we may usefully explore further.

Exploring slow-writing

Choose a word or phrase that you have highlighted from your flow-write. Copy it out at the top of a fresh page. Using this as your heading, write for 20 minutes. You need not write continuously if you want to stop to think. This writing is more consciously focused.

Be open to following different threads, but stay with them a bit longer than in the flow-write. Ask yourself if there is anything else you may have to write on this aspect rather than move on too quickly. In the flow-write, you spread the net wide to catch anything and everything. Now you are examining some of the more interesting and surprising things in your catch.

Afterwards, reread your writing and allow your words to speak back to you. You may wish to retitle this piece. Reflect on where this writing has taken you. If you find it hard to know where to start in your writing, you could repeat the sequence of:

- flow-write;
- reflect and select;
- slow-write.

Exploring different writing modes

Writing, as we have seen, involves formulating what is in our minds into words on the page. Carl Jung identified two aspects of mental processing: taking in information and making decisions about what to do with it. He termed these processes *perceiving* and *judging*.

In writing terms, Jung's two perceiving processes – sensing and intuition – are the sort of writing we do in recording input we have received. His two judging processes – thinking and feeling – relate to writing we do in responding as output, expressing our thoughts or emotions.

The terms sensing, intuition, thinking and feeling may be more familiar as the four mental processing functions of the Myers-Briggs Personality Type Indicator®, which is based on Jung's model. We will look at the writing modes that they highlight in the explanations and exercises below (although, as we shall see in upcoming chapters, our writing may mix them).

Writing our senses

This writing is descriptive – we record what we experience or observe, relying on our senses to tell us what is actually there. It helps us capture a moment to preserve in words. Our own descriptive writing is unique to us – it conveys those particular, specific details that we personally have noticed, even if others have missed them. We note these as faithfully and vividly as we can.

Practising this mode of writing can help us focus more intently on our environment. Gillie Bolton comments that such activity can sharpen our senses, putting us 'in essential contact with the world and others'.[3]

Making fullest use of our God-given senses opens us up to the abundance of life that Jesus promised. It can connect us fully to the present moment, keeping our attention on what we are experiencing right now rather than past regrets or future worries.

A sensing writing exercise

Spend a few minutes using your senses to explore the room around you. Look carefully; listen for what you can hear; move around the room; smell and touch things, feeling their textures. Note the light, time of day and anything else that comes to your sensory awareness.

Take time to notice and observe what is around you as if you are encountering it for the first time. Don't assume you know what is there. Now write for ten minutes, describing what your senses have shown you.

> If I feel fearful or low, I go out into the garden and focus on looking at something – perhaps a leaf or a snowdrop. I may take a photo of it, come back in and use the picture to write about it. This helps re-ground me in the present moment. Christians can often be caught up in the difference between how things are and how they think things ought to be. When things aren't right, we may be quick to feel guilty or sinful. This contemplative writing is about paying attention to what is actually there, with no judgement, or striving to achieve. It reflects the grace that Jesus offers us in the Gospels – that acceptance of how and where we are.
>
> Flow-writing helps me feel fully released to express whatever I want on to the page. I use six-minute flow-writes to gain access to what's below the surface. For me it is a form of prayer. Talking to the blank page is like taking things to God and opening up space to explore things. Prayer is also about listening. Through this writing I listen for what's going on, trusting in the Holy Spirit's presence in my life. *Cilla*

Writing our intuition

This sort of writing reaches beyond what our conscious mind tells us, open to what may surface from a deeper level. We let ourselves write freely, using our imagination without worrying about what is reasonable, relevant or factual. We may find symbols or images coming to mind. This writing loves to explore more intangible truths and possibilities, dreams and visions.

The flow-write exercise is writing in the intuitive mode, as it is not limited by the logical or the literal but ready to discover

22

rich, new connections. Some surprising ideas and insights may emerge.

Tristine Rainer notes that personal intuitive writing is 'a useful device when you sense that you are out of touch with your inner needs'.[4] As we write our faith, this mode may reveal and reconnect us with aspects of ourselves that the Spirit seeks to bring to light.

An intuitive writing exercise

Take some moments to look at the room around you, letting your imagination roam over what is *not* there. How different could this room be? How would you change it into your ideal room, given no practical limitations whatsoever – including transporting it through time and space? You could invent things to put in it. What would your dream room be like?

Write spontaneously for ten minutes about your fantasy room. Let your imagination take flight as you write. Write quickly, listening for inspirations and intuitions that come up, without critiquing them.

Afterwards, read over your piece. Are there any connecting patterns and themes that highlight your own hopes, needs and wishes? Does the writing suggest any steps you could actually take to change your existing room?

Writing from the heart: feeling

In this writing mode we express our immediate emotions. Heart-writing can be intense and raw as we write our strong feelings. It can be a cathartic process as we experience the relief of releasing our emotions on to the page.

This sort of writing may be repetitive. Its highs and lows may seem exaggerated on rereading. We may find ourselves writing in fragments of sentences, with our handwriting becoming a little more uneven as emotion pushes our pen. Finding words for our feelings helps us acknowledge them and give them form. It can be a first step in understanding ourselves and transforming our perspective. Heart-writing can become a pathway that helps us reconnect to self, others and God.

A heart-writing exercise in feeling mode

Choose an issue or dilemma that generates an emotion in you that you want to express in words. Take some moments to bring that feeling into focus as you bring to mind what triggers it.

Now, for ten minutes, express these emotions on paper, writing whatever you feel in response to your chosen issue. Write freely, without being concerned about repeating yourself or having to write in 'proper' sentences. It does not matter – it is the writing process that counts.

Afterwards, take some time to return to calm in the present moment. While this sort of writing is cathartic, and can bring a release of your emotions, it may also potentially stir them up. Allow yourself to settle.

Writing from the head: thinking

In this writing mode we think on paper. This writing is reflective, analytical and contemplative. We step back from our subject to explore it from other points of view and perspectives; consider other arguments, angles and ideas; summarize issues; ask the wondering 'What if?' questions. Its tone may be playful, contradictory or impersonal. It may follow on from other writing modes, which can be vital in helping us use our writing to foster personal change.

Our thinking becomes less rushed and more considered as we write it down. In doing so, we may discover wisdom and answers we did not know we already had, and make space to hear God's 'still small voice' of calm and guidance.

A head-writing exercise in thinking mode

Using the issue you chose for the heart-writing exercise, reflect for a few moments on the triggers that prompted your particular emotion.

Write for ten minutes reflecting on these. You may wish to put some questions to yourself:

- What is it about this issue that specifically touches your emotions?
- Are there any parallels with other situations that stir up this same emotion?

- What does that tell you about yourself?
- What does that tell you about your values?
- Can you discern any underlying factors that contribute to the strength of this emotion?
- What is your attitude towards expressing this emotion as a Christian?

Both feeling *and* thinking are needed to help us change and grow. We may find ourselves moving from one to the other, via a writing mode. At one significant turning point in her life, Anne found that while she did not have to express her feelings on paper, it was helpful to reflect and order her thinking through writing.

> While I was having problems at work, I also became pregnant. I was in a state at my pregnancy check-up. I'd been crying about work. The nurse said I needed to be off work. I didn't want that. I thought that being signed off was for scroungers, but in the end, the doctor signed me off for a month.

During this period Anne found herself very distressed at a particular letter she received from work:

> My husband Steve saw my reaction and became angry at how work was upsetting me. He said, 'Why are you letting things get to you? You're not the person I married.' Then he pointed at the ceiling and said, 'You need help. You're spiritually down. You're not going to church and you're not having your quiet times. Sort that out and the rest will follow.' This was quite a shock. Steve isn't a Christian and professes not to believe in God.

Pulled up short, Anne knew she needed space to absorb what Steve had said.

> His words started the process, but I needed to think things through on paper. I used my journal and ended up writing 'Steve's right. I need to move from head-knowledge to heart-knowledge.' This resulted in me joining a church and gradually reconnecting with my faith.

More things to try

1 Set up your faith-writing, whether in one journal, different books, ring-binder file or on your computer. Will you write under dated entries or separate sections? If the latter, allocate space for your chosen sections. Explore writing at different times and in different locations, to find what works best for you.

2 Look at the list above of what could be included in a Christian journal. Copy it out into two columns, one for writing you have done or do currently, the other for writing you would like to try. Are there aspects of your writing not listed here? What do you like writing most? What sort of writing seems most challenging, and why?

3 As a further sense-writing exercise, choose a devotional activity, such as taking communion or singing a hymn. Draw on all your senses to describe it in vivid, specific detail to someone who has never experienced it.

4 As a further intuition-writing exercise, think about your church fellowship or other group you belong to and see what image forms if you think of it as an animal, a character from a book or film, a sound, a plant – or any other category that occurs to you. For example, you might see it as ivy, clinging on to the church building (would that be a positive or negative image?), or as a cheese-plant, with large wide leaves – open and visible to all. Write about your image, in sentences, or just phrases and ideas. What further connections and associations does it have that might tell you more about how you see this group – its characteristics, strengths and areas for growth?

5 As a further exercise in writing in the feeling mode, read Psalm 133, which proclaims 'How good and pleasant it is when kindred live together in unity!' Where have you felt that unity with other believers? Choose one memorable occasion and write about your feelings at that time, what the experience meant to you and why it was important. You might want to share this experience or the writing with a Christian friend or friends, as an expression of this unity.

6 As a further exercise in writing in the thinking mode, consider an issue where Christians may disagree, whether in the local or wider Church. Write down your own opinions about where you stand and why. Then take the opposite perspective and write as if you held that position. How does the other side understand what is going on? How would they counter your arguments and outlook? Afterwards, reflect on whether writing from another viewpoint has given you any new insights or understanding. Have any conversations or actions emerged from this exercise that might promote better understanding and unity? If so, go and have them, or do them.

3

Plans and prayers

———•◦•———

'Just keep ahead of the man in the chicken suit and you'll be fine', said the svelte, grey-haired woman in the aubergine-coloured running kit. She nodded towards the lumbering yellow figure at the rear of the 6,000 or so runners shuffling towards the start line. It turned out to be good advice for my first ever half-marathon. Nearly two and a half hours later I crossed the finish line outside the Town Hall, astonished to have paced 13 miles – and all without a poultry costume in sight.

If I had prepared for this challenge on my own I would just have tried to run a bit further each time I went out, but Sue, a trainer at my local gym, had different ideas. She set me programmes of exercises to strengthen my muscles and cardio-capacity month by month. I was introduced to 'tempo' running – varying the speed and effort within one run, and shorter spells on the treadmill at different gradients. These exercises sometimes seemed bitty or irrelevant, but they made a surprising difference on days when I did a 'proper' run. I learned not to dismiss the contribution these training elements could make to physical fitness.

It is a lesson I have thought about in relation to other areas of life: the training in godliness that Paul reminds Timothy of is of more value than physical training (1 Timothy 4.7–8); the growth in our capacity to use the writing process.

A complete and polished piece is not the only form of writing that counts as we put pen to paper. Writers also use exercises to develop their writing: jotting down ideas or phrases about something they notice, to work on later; devising brief character sketches; practising observing things; playing with words.

As we write our faith, short exercises can give us a focus and somewhere to start. We can limber up our word muscles, strengthen the links between our faith and its expression in words. In this chapter we will explore some shorter exercises as ways to start writing our faith, from:

- just one word or short phrase;
- writing in threes;
- lists, in all their variety;
- using questions;
- mind-mapping;
- writing our prayers.

Just one word or short phrase

Jesus advised against an abundance of words for their own sake: finely embroidered phrases do not make our prayers more effective (Matthew 6.7). One word can contain all that is needed: as a man in authority, the Centurion who approached Jesus on behalf of his sick servant knew this. All he asked of Jesus was to 'only speak the word, and my servant will be healed' (Matthew 8.8).

As you face the blank page or screen, settle yourself, aware of God's presence. Take a few moments to reflect and, from one of the suggestions below, choose to write:

- a one-word prayer for a particular need;
- one of the names of Jesus;
- a name of someone as a way of remembering that person before God;
- one thing to give thanks for;
- the most significant word you want to characterize your day – such as love, peace;
- two or three words that describe your day (*just* two or three).

Limiting yourself to one word helps to hone down your thoughts to a single focus, cutting away the clutter to record the most important thing. A significant part of the writing process is about what to leave out as well as what to include.

Writing in threes

Writing in threes provides a little more room for manoeuvre within a simple framework. You still need not be daunted at having to write a great deal, but you will need to make some thoughtful choices. Reflecting on what matters enough to include can foster our focus, and we may be surprised to discover what really seems most important to us.

'What do these stones mean?'

Stones can be useful prompts for short pieces of faith-writing. One of several ways in which they hold significance in the Bible is as memorials. When Joshua and the Israelites crossed the Jordan's parted waters into the Promised Land, God instructed them to take 12 stones (for the 12 tribes) from the dried river bed and set them up as a monument at Gilgal, as a permanent reminder of God's powerful activity on his people's behalf (Joshua 4).

Try going outside to find, say, three stones. Bring these back to set up in front of you. Choose from the suggested 'memorials' below to make a threefold list in single words or short sentences:

- three times in your life when God has been especially close;
- three of the most significant steps you have taken forward in faith;
- three of the greatest gifts God has given you;
- three ways God has used you to make a difference;
- three of the biggest thanksgivings in your life.

Writing in threes can help identify what is most significant; your written stones have to earn their place on the page. The process of coming to the decisions that you do is worth reflecting on. What has made these three stones most significant to you?

Lists, in all their variety

From shopping lists to Christmas-card and to-do lists, many of us find this form of writing useful in everyday living. Lists are an accessible and immediate way of capturing information. At a most basic level in writing our faith, some of us use lists to keep track of people or situations to pray for. Although this practice may not suit everyone, the simple list holds a lot of rich potential. Lists can help us:

- remember things;
- catch things in words quickly;
- form notes to explore or work on later;
- help us start writing about a situation if we feel overwhelmed;
- have an aide memoire for prayer;
- summarize the key aspect of a theme, idea, person;
- weigh up options or prioritize issues;
- let go of our immediate feelings;
- draw together different, disparate things;
- express our uniqueness through our choices of what to include.

Lists appear at various points in Scripture. They form elements of God's instructions to his people – for example, the Levitical laws concerning the Israelites' religious, communal and personal life. As Jesus brings the New Covenant, he opens his teaching in the Sermon on the Mount by listing the Beatitudes (Matthew 5.3–11).

Genealogies feature in the Old Testament (1 Chronicles 1—12) and open Matthew's Gospel in the New (Matthew 1.1–16), as the Gospel writer grounds the Incarnation of Christ into God's unfolding plan down the ages. Names unknown to us are recorded as significant for their part in God's purposes.

The sense of being grounded in a story bigger than ourselves is important. It is no accident that in our mobile society, we find people pursuing a greater sense of rootedness as they research their own family trees.

Old Testament lists go beyond straight genealogies. Exodus, for example, catalogues the craftsmen who contributed their gifts and skills to the building of the Tabernacle and Ark and its devotional items, alongside the specific facts and figures of these constructions (Exodus 24—28). There is also the listing of King David's fighting men (1 Chronicles 11.10–47) and his priests, musicians, gatekeepers and other officials, army divisions and tribal officers (1 Chronicles 24—27).

The setting down of a name commemorates the person's deeds for succeeding generations – a practice familiar from our own era from war memorials to plaques listing patrons of charitable projects.

I used to write in organized and neat sentences. Now I'm more relaxed. Since I'm the only one who's going to read it, how I write something does not matter as long as it makes sense to me. When I have troubling or distracting thoughts, I'll write them down – usually in a bullet-point list. Then I choose to put them aside mentally, to be revisited when I can manage them more positively. When I come to do this, the list has already started to provide some structure that makes them easier to process.

My lists can range from the practical to the emotional: what to pack for a holiday; steps involved in clearing an elderly relative's flat; coming to terms with the departure of a vicar whom I've worked alongside as administrator or making sense of angry feelings towards a person or situation.   *Lesley*

Roots and anchors

You could use this principle in your own faith writing by writing a list of roots and anchors. Put these two words as the headings of two columns. Underneath the Roots column, list what has especially rooted you in your Christian life – for example, memories of what God has done in your life; answers to prayer; verses from Scripture that have spoken to you; resources, places and practices that have sustained you.

Underneath the Anchors heading, note down the people who have most anchored you in the ups and downs of your Christian life. Who has been an example to you, someone to turn to, an inspirer or encourager, or perhaps brought you to faith in the first place?

Some of these anchors may not be people you know personally or who have even been alive during your lifetime. It may be their written words or life-stories that have helped you on your way. Writing down people by name is a way of recording their importance and significance in your life. You may wish to reread your list and pray a thanksgiving prayer for each person by name. You may want to add on a prayer of blessing for those you know who are living today, or even write them a short note to thank them for how they have helped you in your Christian life.

Lists for knowing

Lists can be used creatively to review the past or reflect on the present: we can write them for discernment and clarification. Consider writing a list, using one of the following as a prompt:

- Today I felt God was closest when . . .
- Today I felt God was distant when . . .
- Things I did differently today because I am a Christian include . . .
- Things I am grateful to God for include . . .
- I sense my call when I am . . .
- I feel drained when I am . . .

Writing such lists can help focus attention and deepen your awareness of God's presence in the everyday, especially if you begin your day with the conscious intention of writing one of these lists at the end of it. Reading over what you have written can also reveal some useful material or themes to explore prayer further, perhaps in writing.

> Lists are the sticking plasters that keep me in contact with God. I may write a list if I am feeling completely blocked. At times I can feel too distressed or depressed to write, as if I am sitting at the bottom of the pit unable to talk or think. Everything vanishes or goes into a complete blur, and it seems there's no point to anything.
>
> The only way I can deal with that is to write a list of what I have actually done during the day, from the washing to walking to the shops. Then I can say 'thank you' to God for these things.
>
> *Dorothy*

Lists for growing

Lists can also be used in a more future-orientated way: we might expand a basic to-do list beyond the day's tasks to identify longer-term desires and goals. The lists of the gifts and fruit of the Spirit in Paul's letters could also be said to have an aspirational dimension, opening up new possibilities for life and growth.

You may wish to look first at Paul's lists of spiritual gifts, or even copy them out (1 Corinthians 12.8–11). These lists are not exhaustive: as you reflect on them, try writing a supplementary list of further gifts you have noticed being exercised by Christians you know, and use your list as a springboard for thanksgiving prayers.

Reread these lists and choose one of the gifts for further writing and exploration.

- What has drawn you to this particular gift?
- Where can it be most powerfully used – or misused?
- Is this a gift that you recognize you have already been given or have a desire for?

Pray, in words written or spoken, about receiving this gift – or ask your loving heavenly Father for it (Luke 11.9–13) – and offering it back to the Lord for his service.

You could also look at Paul's list of the fruit of the Spirit (Galatians 5.22) and choose the one you identify as closest to your growing edge as a Christian. Write your particular fruit – for example, self-control – at the top of the page, and then use any or all the headings below to prompt your list-writing:

- I see self-control when . . .
- I need self-control most when . . .
- I show self-control most when . . .
- I receive self-control most when . . .

Lists in times of transition

We often make lists in times of transition: moving house, becoming a parent or leaving a job may generate various to-do lists of things to achieve before an ending or to prepare for a beginning. Times of change can be unsettling, and a list can help contain and clarify exactly what needs to be done.

A sense that God is calling us on, or an awareness of changes in ourselves or our circumstances on our Christian life-journey,

can also be disorientating. At such times, you may find it helpful
to use lists to identify:

- what I am letting go;
- what I am taking up;
- what I am struggling to leave behind;
- what I am bringing with me;
- what I am moving towards;
- what is sustaining me through change.

The 'what' in these lists may include people, places, things, routines,
habits, gifts and any other factors important to you. As with the
to-do list, putting these things down on paper encapsulates what
is going on in a way that you can see.

You may wish to give more attention to a specific element
on one of these lists. This could then become a separate head-
line as a prompt for further writing, to express your feelings or
explore your thoughts, taking you deeper into the heart of the
matter.

Listing in different modes

We can write lists in any of the four writing modes introduced
in the last chapter. Compiled in the sensing mode, a written
list may itemize the specifics: jobs to be done, our favourite
things, matters for prayer. King David's writing down of God's
plans for the Temple, and listing of instructions, articles and
measurements, might be said to fall into this category (1 Chronicles
28.11–19).

A list may capture fresh ideas, gather images or jot down possibilities in a more wide-ranging, inventive way. This would be
a list written in an intuitive mode, and may not be numbered
or even written in a column. It is more a creative and colourful
first draft of inspirations than a neat and factually accurate
record.

A list may be more characterized by the feeling writing mode.
Myra Schneider describes 'letting go in lists'[1] as a way of dealing
with her fears and concerns during her period of treatment
for breast cancer. Such a list can help us express our fears and

identify where they are coming from. If we are struggling to define or contain our deeper feelings, it can help to note down what we can in a simple list. This can be a way of bringing these things into God's presence, free of the pressure to articulate them fully. Finding a few words for a feeling, however makeshift or inadequate our words, is a first step in expressing, understanding and ultimately resolving it.

A list may be used to evaluate and analyse a matter. We may be seeking guidance, and want to weigh up the pros and cons of a decision in parallel lists. We may be facing a moral or spiritual dilemma, and want to track the consequences of taking a particular action. This is reflective writing.

Using questions

Questions can also be useful prompts for our writing. They lead most naturally into writing in a reflective mode.

Questioning can work both ways. We may want to list questions we have for God and then explore them.

- What makes them puzzling for us?
- What makes them important to us?
- How might we go about seeking an answer?
- How might we continue to live with the question if the answer is not forthcoming?

Sometimes more heartfelt concerns lie beneath the question we think we are asking. For example, when people going through tough times ask, 'Why me?', the real issue may not be 'Why?' but an underlying anger, disappointment or simply a desperate desire for our pain to stop. As we write around our questions, we may find different issues emerging and find ourselves asking God to meet us at the level of a deeper point of need than we were aware of at the outset.

Two-way questioning

List three questions you would ask Jesus if you met him now. Now choose one of them and write around that question.

- What makes it matter to you?
- What are you really asking?
- What would be an acceptable answer?
- What do you think God's reply to you is?
- How might you go about testing the truth of your assumptions?

In the Bible, God has plenty of questions for human beings too. Read one of the passages containing the questions below as if it were addressed to you, and write your own answer to it.

- 'What are you doing here?' (1 Kings 19.1–9)
- 'Whom shall I send?' (Isaiah 6.1–8a)
- 'What do you want me to do for you?' (Mark 10.46–51)
- 'Who do you say that I am?' (Mark 8.27–29)
- 'Why do you call me "Lord, Lord", and do not do what I tell you?' (Luke 6.46)
- 'Why do you persecute me?' (Acts 9.1–4)
- 'Do you want to be made well?' (John 5.6)

At my 'Writing Our Faith' workshop, Pam found writing her response to Jesus' question, 'Do you want to be made well?' surprisingly difficult.

Pam has a lot on her plate. This energetic and capable volunteer worker in her local parish church also cares for three close family members with long-term health issues.

Pam later told me that she dutifully 'scribbled away, but when I read my writing back, I realized I hadn't looked at what the question really meant to me. I'd just expressed where I was stuck.'

Back home Pam attempted the exercise again. In fact she tried several times to write her answer but got nowhere. More questions surfaced: 'I needed to know my faith was still relevant to my situation', she explained. 'Could it guide and keep me? Who was I and what was my Christian calling?'

This particular writing block prompted Pam to seek further support. Over some months of counselling she faced the challenging realization that while:

I love and care for family members around me, I cannot fix them. They are not mine to fix. My counsellor kept asking me, 'And how are you going to cope with this?' Coming to terms with it all took time. It involved letting go the guilt I felt if I was getting any joy in life, when the rest of the family was in chaos.

We may also ask ourselves questions to explore in writing. They may be as simple as:

- What have I done to fulfil my vocation today?
- What is the most important thing to do next (when you are overwhelmed, needing to take stock and identify just one step ahead)?
- What lies ahead if I continue exactly as I am, in the direction I am going?

Often we will find that God has already spoken to us – once we make space to be attentive to him. The writing process can help slow us down long enough to listen and reconnect with answers already planted within us.

Rather than a question, you could use a simple sentence-opener as a prompt to respond to in a list, phrases, sentences or whole paragraphs. For example:

- I feel afraid when . . .
- My heart's desire is . . .
- I am looking for the Lord in . . .

Mind-mapping

The concept of working with one word can be taken a step further by creating a mind-map (sometimes called 'clustering'). This exercise involves writing down single words or phrases that follow different tracks of thought from a single starting point.

Mind-mapping the word

Clustering can be used as a form of written biblical meditation. Take a Bible passage and read it through slowly, twice. Each time listen out for and be receptive to any particular word or phrase that catches your attention.

After reading the passage through the second time, write the word or phrase that has stayed with you in the middle of a blank page – you might want to turn your page on its side for this.

Now 'map' the word by adding a stem and writing any associated word or phrase that your keyword suggests. Add successive stems, branching out further from the centre as you follow whatever associations or linked words each new one prompts. When you have reached the end of one train of thought, be open to a new word that starts off the next series of stems from your original word or phrase. As with flow-writing, continue without stopping to analyse or filter what comes up. Do not dismiss any idea or link that comes to mind, however tenuous.

Afterwards, read over your mind-map, reflecting on these written fragments. Do you notice any recurring themes? Do any words or connections strike you as especially fresh, insightful or appropriate? You may wish to pick one out to form a new heading on a separate page, and write about it as you meditate on the connection, open to how the Holy Spirit might be underlining some particular insight. You could also record the different insights that have emerged from this exercise by listing them on a fresh page to refer to later.

Mind-mapping the word helped Pam process her concerns:

I kept coming across the verse 'Be still and know that I am God' – in my reading, on a poster, in a sermon. I decided there was something going on here! So I mind-mapped it. I wanted to explore what being still meant for an active person like me.

Pam copied out the verse, underlining each phrase and adding on whatever words came to mind. As she reread her writing, one unexpected word stood out: consistent.

It made me realize that being still is not about doing nothing. It's an active waiting on God. I used to get myself into a heightened state of anxiety, waiting to see what everyone else's mood would be like around me. When I became con-sistent and grounded, it seemed to help others stay calmer. I'm not in control, but my perspective can make a difference to others' behaviour. I've learned a lot from that verse.

Using 'seed' words

This form of mind-mapping can start with your own 'seed' word, enabling you to reflect on something that you may have registered but not fully attended to. This could be:

- a particular emotion you have felt during your day;
- a need;
- a theme of your day;
- a significant moment or event of your day.

Mind-mapping is a meditative rather than analytical activity. It helps to write continuously, but with a sense of gentle rhythm and prayerful receptivity rather than rush. Allow all the words that come up for you on to the page, without judgement or censorship. Not everything will be fruitful, any more than the seeds scattered by the Sower in Jesus' parable would all grow to maturity (Matthew 13.1–8).

Writing our prayers

Finally, if we don't know where to start in our writing, we could begin by writing our prayers. Although not all of us find it helpful to keep a prayer list day-to-day, making a note of what we have prayed about alongside how our prayers have been answered can encourage our faith. Some set up two columns in their journals, writing prayer requests on one side, with the second column blank to write and date the answer that they receive.

The second column may need some space: God's answers to our prayers may not be as simple as ticking a box. Indeed, some Christians have observed that God's answers to our prayers come in at least five different forms:

- Yes!
- No!
- Wait!
- Mind your own business!
- Do it yourself!

Having our original prayer noted down with a space alongside can help us keep track of our prayers and stay committed to taking their outcome seriously – even if that may sometimes feel uncomfortable. If we reread our prayer-list to find one that has not been answered with a straightforward 'yes', we may want to write about this to explore how we understand God to be responding:

- Are we being asked to accept a 'no' or wait for God's *timing* of 'yes'?
- What might indicate this to us?
- Is this a prayer that will not receive an answer we can discern?
- Is there any way in which we are being asked to become at least part of the answer to our own prayers?
- Do we continue to pray this prayer or are we beginning to see this issue from a different perspective?
- Where might that take our praying?

Recording our prayers, either itemized in a list or written out in full, becomes a clear reminder of what we have prayed about. Writing prayers down rather than speaking them out loud or voicing them in your head can be a powerful, patient act of worship. Even if you simply write as you would speak, the very act of writing may make you more mindful and attentive to what it is you want to pray. As Rachel Hackenberg observes, writing prayers 'made praying a whole-body exercise: my creativity was sparked, my spirit fully focused, my muscles employed, my sense of touch and awareness of breath heightened. I felt more connected to prayer than I had ever experienced . . .'[2]

Written prayer brings a substance to our communications with God and is still totally portable. You can write prayers on whatever material is to hand – old envelopes, notebooks, margins of PCC minutes. You can write them wherever you happen to be – on a train, in a coffee shop, at your desk. Written prayers need not be very long – try writing short prayers on postcards or sticky notes. You can take these with you into the day and slip them into a bag or pocket as a way of praying at all times.

Stef has used prayer mind-maps on a big sheet of lining paper, hung on her wall: 'I wrote people's names on it,' she says, 'and then added prayers for them around their names, whenever the need arose.'

She also does the same on A3-sized sheets of paper, taking one for each person or group she wants to pray for and keeping them in a desk drawer: 'It gives me a focus for my prayer and acts as a discipline to pray. I can also go back to these sheets and see what has happened. That's why I write prayers out.'

More things to try

1 Psalm 150 highlights what we could praise God for (v. 2) and what we could praise him with (vv. 3–5). Write your own Psalm-list of what you want to praise God for and the different means you can use to praise him today. These may extend far beyond musical instruments, however many of these you may play.

2 The earlier exercise in this chapter, 'Lists for Knowing', contained two lists that were opposites: times that God felt close versus times that God felt distant. Write two paragraphs, one for each of your lists, drawing together the occasions and common characteristics of when you experienced God close and when he was apparently distant. Now review these two paragraphs to explore the relationship between these two experiences.

- What makes them different?
- Do they have any unexpected connections?
- What has your writing on one side have to say to the other? Write for a few minutes on anything you discern from this reading and reflecting that strikes you as significant.
- Where might this take you?

For example, on the day I did this exercise I realized I had most felt a sense of harmony and well-being in God on getting into the swimming pool and letting all other concerns go to enjoy the feeling of the water. I felt most fragmented and alone when I was amid the clutter of things and unfinished tasks around me in my study at home. In writing I began to wonder if God might release more peace in me if I relaxed into the air of my study in the same way that I'd relaxed into the water of the pool.

4

Writing letters

I got the call as my train pulled out of Crewe. My mother's voice on my mobile phone wavered as she told me my father had just died in his sleep in hospital. He had been rushed in with breathing problems 48 hours earlier, and I was already on my way down south to see him. Now I was travelling into very different territory.

My father had been contending with oesophageal cancer for around two years. Despite my regular visits during that period, I felt I had largely failed in my attempts to talk with him about the deeper issues underlying the surface of the everyday.

My childhood memories of my father were happy. It was only in growing up that I encountered his essentially private character. Childhood affection was succeeded by a more formal adult relationship. Now I felt sad. The last opportunity for heartfelt conversation before our parting had gone.

Going through my father's affairs over the next few days, however, I made an astonishing discovery: a letter to him from me, tucked away in his filing cabinet. In it, I told him how much I appreciated him as a father when I was a child; how I remembered with gratitude our doing things together from jigsaws to early morning holiday swims; his faithful attendance at every school concert that I took part in; the treat of an outing to my first Promenade concert.

Memories of the letter that I had forgotten writing gradually resurfaced. I'd attended a course on Christian relationships around ten years earlier, where we had been encouraged to write a letter of appreciation to someone special. Although my father never spoke to me directly about receiving it, my mother later said my letter had greatly touched him. He had never thrown it away.

Amid my sorrow and self-criticism about so many missed opportunities for deeper conversation with my father, I realized that perhaps I had not been as remiss as I assumed. The letter had helped me communicate what might have been too difficult and embarrassing to express as effectively face to face.

Rereading the letter, I realized I had nothing more to add. The key things I was grateful for – my father's active input into my formative years – had been affirmed. Knowing this brought a sense of peace and completion. I was aware of God's merciful provision, the importance of letters and the relief of having written this one when I did.

Letters

Since technology opened the floodgates of communication via email, Facebook, Twitter and text, the handwritten letter has become a rarity within a generation. In 1987, a United States Postal Service survey revealed that the average American household received a personal letter once a fortnight. In a comparable survey carried out in 2011, it was down to one personal letter every seven weeks. Although this does not include notes people have written in cards for special occasions such as birthdays, the number of greeting cards being sent is itself in decline.

'Write letters. It's a dying art', an Elim church pastor recalls his mentor telling him as he trained for ministry in the early 1980s. 'A handwritten letter can have a profound impact.'

Christians, of all people, should be attuned to the impact of letters: 21 of the 27 New Testament books are in letter form, 13 of them written by Paul. Some of those remaining, such as Acts and Revelation, also contain letters.

Apart from his personal, pastoral epistles to Timothy, Titus and Philemon, Paul and his fellow New Testament letter-writers – Peter, John, James, Jude and the writer to the Hebrews – addressed their letters to the fledgling fellowships springing up across Asia Minor in the wake of Paul's missionary journeys. These would be read aloud to a whole congregation.

The addressing of a group rather than an individual was just one factor contributing to a New Testament letter's more formal feel. Letter-writing in those days involved a significant expense of paper, ink and time. A letter would be composed carefully and expressed concisely. Its conventional layout included opening with the sender's name, with greetings to the recipient left to the end – the reverse of our practice today.

Within this structure such letters were the next best thing to a face-to-face encounter with their authors. They kept relationships alive and were treasured by a generation of believers who did not yet have written Gospels to look to.

The New Testament letters fulfilled a variety of purposes. Paul writes as a theologian, teaching the Romans, but as more of a pastor to the Corinthians. He encourages the Philippians but exhorts the Galatians. James writes with practical guidance, while Peter's letters 'envision' – by which I mean energize and inspire with hope – a Church suffering persecution.

These letters were treasured and copied for wider circulation. Ultimately, of course, they gained a readership across time as well as distance. Included in the Christian Scriptures, they have had an impact far beyond anything their original authors could have imagined.

Christians in subsequent generations have been prolific letter-writers. In the second half of the fourth and fifth centuries, Christian letter-writing enjoyed a particular flourishing – for example, the abbot and ascetic St Isadore of Pelusium, in Egypt, was known to have written around 10,000 letters during his lifetime. Some 2,000 of these, which offer teaching, encouragement and comfort as well as reproach, have survived to this day.

We may feel our humble correspondence is small fry compared to the canon of Scripture and the great heritage of letter-writing Christians down the ages, yet our letters can play their own small but significant part in God's purposes. Our own words, composed with prayer and love, may be treasured to an extent that would surprise us.

We can write letters for many reasons, such as to:

- share news;
- offer encouragement;
- convey concern;
- request prayer;
- express love or appreciation;
- say thank you;
- apologize and ask for or offer forgiveness;
- communicate an answer to prayer;
- pass on an insight or word of wisdom;
- draw attention to a piece of Scripture.

Handwritten letters are personal and their words have a quality of permanence. They can also be very precious. Some people keep particularly special letters in the back of a journal or Bible. I have a folder designated for cards or letters that have made a positive impact on me and that I want to treasure. They form a personal library of encouragement for the tough times.

Four years ago we did a church activity where we wrote things we appreciated about one another on pieces of paper on one another's backs. Afterwards a lady in our congregation wrote to me as her Pastor and said she did not have space to put what she had wanted to on mine. So she went home and wrote them all out as a list.

They were in the form of an alphabet, each quality beginning with a different letter from A for Appreciative through to Z for Zealous. Each one had a sentence explaining her choice, so there was Q for Questioning, 'but never inquisitive'.

She wrote that she hoped this 'A to Z of You' would encourage me whenever I was down, as 'pastors need encouragement', and that 'The Holy Spirit is lovely. He knows what we should say.'

This is a unique piece of writing. I keep it in the back of my Bible, and although this lady has since died, her words continue to bless me.

Nigel

The printed word can also make a powerful impact. I have also printed off and kept several emails that have especially touched and helped me. One is folded into the back of my journal; another, pinned to my study notice-board, was written by someone who felt they sensed God was calling me to take my writing in a particular direction, and who dared to pass this on gently and respectfully. The writer's words continue to inspire and focus the writing I do.

What can we write today that will bless someone and build them up? Our written words can have a lasting effect, and we are not limited to offering them within our church, family or friendship circles.

Recently we had some excellent service from a hard-working young waiter. I wrote a brief letter to the restaurant manager to express our appreciation. When we revisited the restaurant a few months later, the waiter recognized us and said how the letter had not only encouraged him but also played a part in helping him increase his working hours and employment prospects.

In our busy culture of complaint and compensation, taking the time to express genuine appreciation where it is due can also be a significant witness. We can freely affirm others with no expectation of return.

About that email . . .

Although there is something especially personal in the gift of a handwritten letter or note on a well-chosen card, this is not to denigrate the use of modern digital media as a way of blessing others through our written words.

A text to someone who is ill, which may simply be to pass on a Bible verse that has come insistently to mind in your prayers for that person (you do not need to know why!), can be a wonderful sustainer that is not too demanding for an ill person to access and absorb.

The major advantage of writing over talking, however, is that it offers greater opportunity to reflect on what you want to say. An instant communication facility has a tendency to speed up the process. This may work well for a brief, straightforward note, but there is a danger that an email can be too hastily 'fired off' without due care and attention.

Emails and texts are also more easily open to misinterpretation. They are often categorized as being halfway between a letter and a phone call or face-to-face conversation. As their authors, we may hear our words in our heads as we type, including the tone in which we are speaking, but this does not appear on the screen. Readers are faced with bare text, unaccompanied by the vital clues of our tone of voice or facial expression. They may fill in the blanks by projecting their own anxieties on to our words.

Print also carries a certain authority. Typed words can come over more strongly than their authors realize – what we wrote as direct may be received as attacking; our humorous comment or tease can seem more heavy-handed than we intended.

Emoticons or animated smileys within your text may help. Using an emoticon – a portmanteau word comprising emotion and icon – to nuance words with mood goes back to the 1850s, when 73 became the Morse code abbreviation for 'best regards'. In 1982 the American Professor Scott E. Fahlman suggested using the punctuation constellation : -) to soften internet communications with a smile. Emoticons have developed into a widely recognized element of internet language.

It is also worth remembering the Drafts folder, which enables you to save a message and sleep on it. An objective read-through with fresh eyes the next day may alert you to a change you need to make before your missive passes the point of no return through the Outbox. Whatever your final version, it can be useful to develop the discipline of 'pray before press' as your fingers prepare to click on Send. : -)

Unsent letters

At various times I have counselled clients experiencing bereavement. Sometimes I have suggested that they write an unsent letter to the loved one they have lost. This tends to generate one of two responses. Some are eager to try it, and come back to report how surprisingly powerful they found the exercise. For others, it is a non-starter: 'What's the point of that?' I've been asked, 'The person's dead.'

But writing unsent letters in such circumstances is not about contacting the dead. The point is to help the living work through their loss. If we find it hard to verbalize our grieving emotions spontaneously with other people, a quiet, uninterrupted space, the privacy of the page and the writing process can be particularly helpful.

Writing can enable us to find words for our feelings and thoughts, to give some shape to what is swirling around within. This can help us reorientate ourselves amid grief's confusions. It can also help us release our sorrows in a safe place, so that sadness does not become locked inside, weighing us down to imprison us in depression.

Writing in this form – addressing our words to our lost, loved ones – can also transform and resolve our relationship with them. It can allow elusive memories of the person to surface and be acknowledged. This can help us reconnect with aspects of that person that we treasure and want to carry with us always. I have also heard people talk of gaining a new insight or fresh perspective on their loved one and their relationship to them that they were not aware of during the person's lifetime.

My sceptical clients are right: an unsent letter to a lost loved one will not change the situation. But it can help release, revitalize and heal us as we move along the pathway towards a settled completion of our grieving in coming to terms with our loss.

Loss is not the only context for this form of writing. An unsent letter to someone living can be used to help restore a good relationship or resolve a difficult one; to diffuse a situation or prepare us to face it.

We may know that our feelings are running high, and could drive our tongue in saying something unloving or out of turn. We may sense that our anxiety about a particular face-to-face encounter might stop our tongue altogether from saying what needs to be said. We may have an issue with someone who is unavailable to speak to, or who is unaware of any issue from our side.

In all these instances, an unsent letter can be a practical response to the warning in James' letter about the risks of doing damage with our tongue, through the destructive potential of the spoken word (James 3.2–10). We may protect others and ourselves from inflaming a situation or causing unnecessary hurt by diverting passionate feelings and negative thoughts down a safer channel.

An unsent letter may be written to:

- someone who has caused you distress;
- someone who has angered you;
- someone from your past with whom there is unfinished business;
- someone you are about to face in a difficult encounter;
- someone who unwittingly raises issues personal to you alone;
- someone you do not know personally but with whom you would take issue.

Writing an unsent letter is best enfolded by prayer before and behind. The object of the exercise is not to indulge negative feelings and attitudes but to discharge and resolve them. However, you do not need to fear expressing them: God will see no surprises appear on the page, even if you do. As you continue to write freely, you may find that releasing the layer of raw feelings and wild thoughts through your pen may not only enable you to reach a new perspective but also open the way for the Holy Spirit to bring comfort and wisdom about your best way forward.

Where something still needs to be addressed directly with the person concerned, an unsent letter may strengthen you in setting aside what you feel like saying to identify what needs to be communicated in a more constructive and loving way. In so doing you are more likely to be heard: a quiet word can often be more penetrating than a loud shout.

We can be rightly angered at wrongs, and in his letter to the Ephesians, Paul exhorts Christians to speak the truth to one another. But he also urges us not to let anger control us (Ephesians 4.26). An unsent letter may help us allow God to stay in charge.

Some guidance for writing unsent letters

- Ensure that you are in a private, uninterrupted and quiet place to write.
- Invite the Holy Spirit to release what needs to come out.

- Give yourself permission to write freely, exactly as you feel. God already knows what is in your heart.
- Keep writing beyond the point where you feel you have anything to say. Sometimes it is in writing through and beyond the point of pain that key insights and transformations can happen.
- Afterwards, read over what you have written. You may want to put the letter away and come back to it later before doing this.
- As you reread, invite the Holy Spirit to highlight what is important, to help you filter out and let go of what is not.
- Ask the Holy Spirit for the next step – a letter that you do send, a conversation, prayer, a leaving things be?
- Unsent means unsent. Store your letter in a safe place if you intend to keep it. You may prefer to tear it up to express your freedom from the issues it represents.

Letters to God

The Jerusalem post office has a special box in its dead-letter room for undeliverable mail. The box is labelled 'Letters to God', and is designated for the 1,000 or so letters that arrive each year addressed to God in Jerusalem. Every few months, these are opened and their contents folded. The letters are then taken to be pressed into the cracks of the Wailing Wall of Jerusalem's Temple.

Websites such as Our Letters to God[1] and Letters to God[2] invite you to post and publish your own letters as well as read those of others. Letters to God has received 30,000 letters since being set up in 2005. Its highest-ranking topic categories are Help, Desires and Family.

Whether a letter to God is posted in a letter box or website or remains unsent, it always reaches its intended recipient. God can read our hearts even before we express our innermost life on paper and invite him to share it.

Writing a letter to God can be helpful to us, even if it initially feels like a one-sided conversation. Through it, we can clarify our concerns and what exactly we are trying to say to God in our prayers. It also reminds us of the relational heart of our faith. We write directly and personally to the God who calls us his children.

Young children's letters to God, of course, have sometimes been published. Their honesty and unvarnished directness, as in 'OK, God, I kept my part of the bargain. Now where's the bike?' has contributed to their popular appeal.

If we are honest with ourselves, some of the letters raise smiles as we recognize how they voice the sorts of issues we have with God ourselves. The only difference is our reluctance to disclose what we fear might be judged as unholy, improper or selfish, although the Jerusalem post office did receive one fortune-hunting letter to God that alerted the almighty to the sender's lottery ticket numbers.

What would you write to God if you knew that you only, and no one else from church, would see it? How different would it be from what you are willing to voice out loud? You may be prompted to write a letter to God to:

- ask for guidance;
- ask for help for yourself or another;
- ask questions about things that puzzle or distress you;
- tell God how you feel about him;
- say thank you for something;
- express your feelings;
- express your response to a particular situation.

It is important to write freely as you want, not as you 'ought'. Your setting needs to be private and you need to allow yourself enough time not to feel rushed. Write for as long as you are in the flow and able to keep continue writing.

When you have finished your letter, reread it – not necessarily right away. Reflect on what has emerged. You may have found yourself writing things that surprised you.

How do you address God and what does that indicate about how you are relating to him? Does the letter change as it goes on? If so, compare this to writings in the psalms, such as Psalm 13, where the writer starts in one frame of mind as he expresses himself freely to God but ends with a changed outlook. Has the same happened to you?

It is worth keeping your letter, perhaps in your journal or Bible. You may want to revisit it at some point, to consider how you

have moved on, how God has answered you, and what remains
unresolved.

> It started without me really planning it. I was on holiday and
> got up early one morning and sat outside our cottage. The sun
> was shining, birds were singing. Creation looked beautiful. So
> I just started a letter, Dear God, and wrote and said thank you
> for bringing us here and about how lovely it was. I've kept that
> letter and have written others since. It goes in phases.
>
> I wrote a series of letters when my husband Keith was
> diagnosed with cancer, throughout the course of his illness,
> operation and recovery. I sometimes found it very difficult at
> that time to formulate a prayer, so putting it all down on paper
> was very helpful. Sometimes I was asking lots of questions;
> other times I was just asking for strength, courage, peace, and
> above all healing. I also wrote thank-you letters as the situation
> developed. It's useful to look back at a later date, and realize
> that God has replied, very often 'in spades'.   *Patricia*

What would Jesus write?

It was Sunday morning at the Christian conference. Crowds were
making their way towards the morning worship venue. As I drifted
dutifully along in their wake, I realized that I really did not want
to be there. My mind was buzzing with threads and impressions
of how I felt God had spoken to me over the last few days, but
I could not grasp their shape with any clarity. Brushing off the
temptation to guilt, I turned against the tide of people to search
for my journal, Bible, pen and a quiet space. Already I felt a sense
of relief.

I sat down with my journal but did not know where to start
or how to settle all my inner mental chattering into something
approaching silence. I needed some active way of listening. And
then I had it. Suppose God were to write a letter to me? What
would he say?

I prayed that the Holy Spirit would keep me in tune with what
God would write to me, and then wrote, right down to the end

of the page and more. Some things came easily and quickly to mind, but as I kept writing, it felt as if I was moving down into the deeper layers beyond my reach in the busyness of activity. Phrases and insights emerged. One or two surprised me; I kept on writing.

When I prayed and reread the letter afterwards, particular sections, often the more 'surprising' ones, began to resonate. They were consistent with Scripture and they crystallized things that had felt confused. I wrote up the letter more neatly in my journal and still have it. Two years on, some of those phrases continue to speak.

This activity was different – neither automatic writing nor 'getting in touch with the wise self'. It was more, as a Christian, a way of paying attention to what the indwelling Holy Spirit, the comforter and guide, was already saying but which was getting muffled out by outer distraction and preoccupation. Writing a letter from God helped me to slow down enough to hear these things more clearly. My initial surprise was followed by a sense of recognition about some of what I had written.

Generally speaking, God is more interested in speaking to us and guiding us than we are to listening to him and receiving his direction. This exercise can help release those things he has already said to us but that have become a little buried in our consciousness.

Whatever we do feel we are to take on board in our Letter from God needs also to be held up to the light of Scripture as a further check on the accuracy of our hearing. Not everything we write as from God will be right, or even of special significance. This sort of letter can also benefit from a prayerful revisiting after a longer period of time. It may then be even more clear which parts you may want to circle or underline as at the heart of God's communication to you.

God does not speak without purpose but wants to enable us to grow up in him. As you reflect on this piece of writing, consider the implications of responding to what you sense as the Holy Spirit's authorship. Is there something you need to start or stop doing? A situation to address? A new awareness of yourself in Christ or a particular aspect of him that you need to bear in mind?

Guidelines for a letter from God

- Find a private and uninterrupted space.
- Have paper, pen, Bible – and maybe a cup of tea – to hand!
- Take some moments to settle yourself.
- Ask the Holy Spirit to protect the writing and speak clearly through it.
- Write the letter freely, continuing to write beyond what you think there is to say. It may be that when your mind has run dry, the Spirit's words can flow.
- Review prayerfully after a cooling-off period.
- Test what you have written against Scripture.
- Continue to pray through significant sections carefully, particularly where there are actions you may sense you are being called to take in response.

More things to try

1 Take the time to write a handwritten letter of encouragement or appreciation to someone special. Give careful, prayerful thought not only to your words but to your choice of paper or card and the pen you use.

2 Could you write an alphabet of appreciation for someone special in your life, beginning each quality you want to highlight with the next letter of the alphabet? Don't be inventive; do be creative!

3 Write an unsent letter to someone in your past or present with whom you have some issue that is unresolved.

4 Write a letter to God. Seek to approach God as his child – honest, open, trusting and vulnerable. One way of doing this can be to write the letter with the hand you do not usually use to write.

5 Write a letter from God to you. What might he already be saying to you that this exercise could unearth? The letter from God

may open our conscious minds to what the Holy Spirit has already imprinted on our hearts.

6 The next time you meet good service or help in your daily life, don't keep your gratitude to yourself. Write a brief letter to make this known to the person or to an appropriate person within their workplace. The letter does not have to be long, but be as specific as possible about what aspect of service was especially helpful.

5

Stories

————◆◆◆————

'God created people because he loves stories'. So says a Yiddish proverb. If that is so, our human love of stories reflects our being made in God's image. We may tell stories around a campfire or type them on to a computer screen; listen to a stand-up comedian or a pulpit preacher; immerse ourselves in Dickens or *EastEnders*. Wherever we tell them in our digitally connected, information-rich society, stories retain their power to make that information alive and open up heart-to-heart communication.

We exchange stories in our everyday life all the time: how the interview went; my dreadful car journey through the snow; exploits of my pet; that embarrassing incident in church.

Last night I was at an independent publisher's lecture. A potentially dull talk about sales and statistics came alive as he regaled us with tales – the writer who sent off his manuscript under a supposedly more appealing Irish pseudonym, only to have to spend months faking a convincing accent in phone calls with the interested agent; the publicist who filled every shelf in a bookshop with a copy of the same book to promote its launch.

Although I was itching to recount the stories I'd heard to my husband as soon as I got home, I thought that my tiredness or his might lessen their impact. So I saved them up until morning and went to sleep smiling in the dark at the prospect of laughter over the breakfast toast and coffee.

Think about stories in your own life. How far back do you have to go to recall the last story you told?

- To whom did you tell it?
- What made you choose to tell it – both why and when?

- Was it a story of your own experience or one you had heard, read or seen?
- Was it a true story?
- Were you conscious of colouring, editing or reshaping it in your telling?
- From whose point of view were you telling it?

Stories are a key element in our human expression and relationships. We instinctively sequence incidents of our day into stories to tell each other at teatime; we pass stories down through generations in our communities. Most of us have stories in our family or friendship circles that are regularly retold to our delight, embarrassment or both. When my mother-in-law mistook the mayonnaise for cream, which she generously poured over portions of chocolate roulade, the result was an unforgettable taste experience and an enduring story still recalled at family gatherings. Stories have the power to:

- entertain us;
- encapsulate an experience;
- bring shape to apparently disconnected events;
- unite a group;
- stir our emotions;
- connect us to the teller;
- reveal our character;
- affirm our outlook – or challenge our thinking and assumptions;
- shift our perspective;
- bring fresh understanding or insight;
- prompt a change in our behaviour;
- spiritually enrich us.

In this chapter we will look at the place of story in the Bible, the stories we create, our own life stories and the stories that shape us.

When it comes to the Bible, 'Stories hold pride of place in revealing God and God's ways to us', according to the writer and theologian Eugene Peterson.[1] Although, as we noted earlier, it comprises various genres of writing, Peterson reminds us that 'The

Bible is basically and overall a narrative, an immense, sprawling, capacious narrative.'

God's word to us is his story writ large. It tells of his relationship with all he has made, opening with his act of creation itself, closely followed by the fall of humankind. The plot develops as God seeks to draw us back to himself, ultimately offering salvation through his Son's earthly life, death and resurrection. The story ends anticipating the climax of Christ's return and Creation's renewal – the opening of a new chapter in an ever-unfolding sequel.

Tributaries of smaller stories flow into this mighty narrative river. There are stories of community and nation: God's calling of a special people to represent him on earth; their faith, frailty and failures in response; the fate of Israel and Judah amid a succession of surrounding empires; the group of disciples who followed Jesus and the communities of the early Christian Church.

Within this are individuals' stories – most supremely the Gospel stories of Jesus, whose life and ministry forms the lynchpin of the whole narrative. There are stories of the journeys of patriarchs; trials of prophets; deeds of Kings; one-to-one encounters with Jesus and the adventures of the first generations of Christians.

Bible characters themselves communicate through story. Jesus tells parables, as do the prophets. Nathan calls King David to account about his adultery with Bathsheba by telling him a story (2 Samuel 12.1–12). When Solomon is faced with two mothers claiming parentage of the same infant, he uses their response to a story to elicit the truth (1 Kings 3.16–28).

Some try to control events using false stories. Potiphar's wife creates fictions about Joseph's advances (Genesis 39.13–30). Matthew's Gospel recounts how religious leaders try to scotch rumours of Jesus' resurrection by bribing Roman soldiers to circulate the tale that the disciples stole his dead body from the tomb (Matthew 28.12–15).

A story's power to affect its hearers' thinking and behaviour may be abused to manipulate others, but it is still the case that a good, honest story invites the listener's response. Eugene Peterson asserts that 'stories are verbal acts of hospitality', and that the

Bible's stories ultimately 'invite us into this large story that takes place under the broad skies of God's purposes'.

> I write short stories of around 2,000 words, usually based on New Testament encounters with Jesus. For me it's a creative way of entering the Bible story and reflecting on what's going on. For example, I looked at the woman who'd been bleeding for 38 years and spent all she had. I focused on that word 'spent' and on how she felt – what she longed for in her meeting with Jesus. I look at the commentaries, but not when I'm actually writing. I move from the text to my imagination. I imagine what's going on in the character and 'around the corners' of the story.
>
> My mind has to be in a spacious sort of a place to do this – on retreat, away from the parish, or when I can take myself aside from the daily tasks. This activity releases something in me that nothing else does. I tend to discover a joy in Jesus and a playfulness that I think is in tune with the text. Using my imagination helps me notice things that are not immediately obvious. Sometimes I feel I've discovered something through the story that is worth sharing with others, unlike my journal, which is private.
>
> *Ricarda*

Continuing in the story

As we put our trust in how the Bible makes sense of the world around us, we start to live under the authority of its story. We allow its meaning to shape our outlook, understanding and actions so that it becomes Christ's story in us and ours in him.

Christian testimonies are the stories of those who have responded to God's invitation to join his story. They can inspire faith, encourage others and build unity between believers. They can also deepen our understanding of who God is and how he works.

Written testimonies form a permanent record of personal faith journeys that can be told down generations: in the 1420s the colourful character Margery Kemp dictated an account of her pilgrimages across Europe and to the Holy Land to scribes who wrote *The Book of Margery Kempe* – seen by some as the first autobiography in the English language. In the later twentieth century, Jackie Pullinger, another woman of faith whose call took her on a long journey, wrote about her experience of ministering to drug addicts in Hong Kong's Walled City in *Chasing the Dragon*.

Writing our testimony involves giving it a structure and story ingredients: beginning, middle and end; main character; setting; a dramatic momentum of challenges faced and overcome. It brings order to a journey already taken, with some resolution of difficulties confronted on the way. The writer will have made choices about what to put in or leave out and which events are most significant, looking back. Stories are also told in contracted time, a passing of years sometimes covered in a sentence.

By comparison, our own faith struggles may seem to go on for a long time. We may feel stuck in a muddle in the middle of our living story, the longed-for 'happy ever after' ending frustratingly out of reach.

Although we need to be honest about our vulnerability at faith's front line, writing our faith-story, even in part, may help us see how far we have come and how God has been with us on the way. It may also help prepare us to tell our unique story of faith to others. The apostle Peter urges Christians to be ready to give 'an account of the hope that is in you' (1 Peter 3.15). Writing our faith-story can:

- help us see a thread through what might seem a random series of events;
- enable us to identify significant turning points;
- prepare us to tell our story more effectively to others;
- strengthen our faith;
- prompt our gratitude;
- help us see ourselves through Christ's compassionate eyes;
- change our perspective to appreciate God's bigger picture;
- deepen our understanding of who God is and how he acts;
- suggest an underlying direction in which we are being guided.

A good story does not include every single detail. It leaps over some sections to linger over the significant events and action that move it on. Identifying these elements can help us structure our own story. To help you do this, try the following exercise:

Telling our story: interactions

Take your own faith journey or choose one particular aspect or season of it to track. At the top of your page write a sentence or phrase noting your starting point, and at the bottom another sentence headlining a point of completion.

Reflect on your progress from start to end, writing each significant stage down the page in a short sentence or phrase. Each stage will mark a time when God's presence interacted with you on your journey, when his guidance, word, an event, place, circumstance, experience, action of another, personal decision or deep conviction provided a turning point or impetus to move onward. Be open to discovering an interaction that may have seemed incidental at the time but that you now realize is significant as you look back.

Reread your list and circle the most significant interactions from start to end. Try to have no more than five. Ensure these are in chronological order.

Now choose one interaction to write about in more detail, using your short sentence or phrase as an opener. Include who you were and where you were at that time. Describe what and how things changed as precisely as you can. A paragraph may be enough – you may find yourself writing more but try to stay within 300 words.

Repeat with the other interactions. Expand your starting point to form an introduction and your end point to an outcome. You may prefer to spread this activity over several sessions rather than do it all at once.

Next, write a sentence or two between each interaction, to stitch these episodes into one story. Aim for a complete version not exceeding 1,500 words, which may mean some trimming. The different parts may vary in length.

The average speaking pace for audio books is around 150–160 words per minute, so you now have a ten-minute story to tell.

Now imagine you have just a five-minute-slot and rewrite your testimony at half its length – 750 words. This will discipline you to make decisions about your story's essentials. It is harder to write a shorter piece than a longer one, but you may be surprised at how much your piece gains from some resolute editing. Your final five-minute written faith-story forms both a personal record and potential testimony of God's work in your life.

Take some moments to reflect on this exercise, perhaps writing down your thoughts. Has writing your story given you fresh insights into your life's shape and direction under God's hand? Did other interactions come to mind during this process? A further challenge comes at the end of the chapter.

Exploring stories

It started when I wanted to make Bible stories alive for my children. I have a vivid imagination. I like to imagine how people look and the reasons they do things as I shape stories. But I wanted to write a story of my own.

I found a story starting to grow in my head. I'm immersed in Scripture, so it has Christian themes – the spiritual battle between good and evil. It's a children's novel, and it took me six years to write. I started with the character and the ending, but needed to let the middle bit evolve.

If I got stuck, I'd go for a consciously prayerful walk and imagine 'What if . . . ?' You use your experience and imagination to form something, just like God loves to do with us. He draws creativity out of you and helps you grow.

I've learned a lot through writing this story. Most of all, I've found I can write a book. I thought I couldn't achieve this. Don't put God in a box and limit what he can do. He is a creative God, and when we go to heaven, he will still be creative and so will we.

Lynn

We not only tell our own stories, we also create stories to tell. Stories structure events to bring both shape and meaning. The most effective stories, as we have noted, offer that meaning by inviting – rather than coercing – us to respond. We have space to draw our own conclusions and perhaps change in some way as a result.

Jesus engaged his listeners' hearts, attention and imagination with such stories. He told stories about characters they would recognize, from Pharisee to tax collector, father to farmer. He used illustrations from his listeners' worlds, whether agricultural, political or religious. He told stories in response to questions and then turned the question back to his listeners, as with the parable of the Good Samaritan and its underlying question, 'Who is my neighbour?' (Luke 10.29–37).

Jesus' stories could entertain, provoke or challenge. They overturned assumptions and opened windows into the kingdom of God for those willing to look.

Reflect on the parables Jesus told. Which one can you recall most easily right now? You may want to reread it. Consider:

- What makes this story memorable to you?
- When did you first hear it or remember hearing it?
- What impact has it had on you?
- What is the story's 'punchline' or point?
- Have you changed something as a result?
- Do you need to change something as a result?
- How did Jesus' listeners respond?
- Why do you think Jesus told it?
- To which character are your sympathies drawn?

Now rewrite this parable for present-day listeners. The original provides the story's structure, but who will be your characters? What setting would be familiar to twenty-first-century hearers in a Western culture? Does anything else need to change? How can you keep the impact of the parable's point?

For Graham, a vicar, the obvious parable to choose for this exercise was the Parable of the Talents. He says he finds this story memorable as it reminds him that 'Jesus calls us to be risk-takers', using and investing the resources God has given. He feels that churches can find this something of a challenge. Graham's modern version of the parable has the flavour of the television show *The Apprentice*, as a company executive goes off to manage a new business venture, leaving his business in the hands of chosen employees.

Your modern-day parable need not be very long (Jesus' stories weren't). It may follow the original very closely or need some storyteller's licence to link it more effectively to contemporary culture. However satisfied you feel with the result, doing this writing exercise will help you engage more deeply with the story and its meaning. You may wish to try the exercise with others, to share ideas and insights about how to update the parable most effectively.

> Telling stories about something always helps me to understand the world. The story can be a testing ground for real life. It asks 'What if . . . ?' Most good stories have a mustard seed of truth in there. You get to recognize its taste.
>
> When I am working on retelling a story from Scripture, I start by identifying its theme and who I'm going to tell it to. I also need to decide who will be the main character.
>
> In the Parable of the Good Shepherd, it could be a sheep or the shepherd. The way into shaping a story based, say, on Jesus' comparing the kingdom of heaven to a pearl of great price might be from the point of view of a pearl merchant or the pearl's finder.
>
> Approaching a story from a different viewpoint reveals new things about it. I might explore its connections by writing a mind-map as I pray and reflect on it. This helps me come to an understanding of how I see the story.   *Amy*[2]

Some Christians have turned to fiction to explore issues of faith. John Bunyan's allegory *The Pilgrim's Progress*, published in 1678, is the imaginative tale of Christian's challenging journey 'from this world to that which is to come'. Part of its enduring popularity is in how it resonates with common experience. As the commentator Macaulay observed, 'Every reader knows the strait and narrow path as well as he knows a road on which he has been backwards and forwards a hundred times.'

Bunyan, a non-conformist churchman in prison for preaching outside the Anglican fold, wrote the book in Bedford County Jail. His few possessions, apart from a Bible and a flute made from a chair leg, included pen and paper.

William P. Young's contemporary novel, *The Shack*, also explores a personal faith issue, in this case why God seems to allow suffering and evil to go unchecked. In Young's story, Mack's journey in coming to terms with his young daughter Missy's abduction and murder involves an encounter with the Trinitarian God presented in imaginative human form.

The book was originally a piece of personal writing – a Christmas gift for Young's six children. Close friends persuaded him to publish it. The book has now sold over 18 million copies, its popularity spread initially by word of mouth. Something in it has struck a chord for many. Young says that the abandoned woodland shack, where Missy's bloodied clothing is found, stands for 'the house you build out of your own pain . . . the place you get stuck, you get hurt, you get damaged'.

Living whose story?

Everyday stories can affect our outlook or actions: a tale of a dodgy plumber; a newspaper story about immigration; the office gossip about a work colleague. How much we allow these to direct us depends on our trust in the storyteller's authority and motives.

We also have stories we tell ourselves, about ourselves and who we are in the world.

As Christians who trust God's love and power, we want to let God's story shape our lives, but sometimes other people's stories can get in the way. Stories we have been told about who we are by significant adults past and present can affect us in healthy or unhelpful ways.

- Describe an incident from your everyday life involving another person or people that left you feeling fulfilled, positive or grateful to God in some way.
- Describe an incident from your everyday life involving another person or people that left you feeling frustrated, dissatisfied or stuck in some way.

Write your reflections on the incidents you have written.

- What is it about who you are and how you and others act in the first one that makes it positive?
- What aspects of God's story in you does it affirm?
- What is it about who you are and how you and others act in the second incident that makes it more negative?
- Whose expectations and what beliefs are obscuring God's story in you?
- Are you playing, or trying to play, a particular role, such as victim, people-pleaser, conflict-avoider, fixer, diva, hero, underdog?

We may become aware of living an unhelpful story when life feels stuck or especially draining. As in the film *Groundhog Day*, where the main character, meteorologist Phil Connors, finds himself waking up on 2 February morning after morning, we may find ourselves reliving the same frustrating situations; relationship patterns; stresses; arguments that go nowhere.

Look back at the positive incident you have described. You may wish to celebrate this story with your own prayer of thanksgiving for how it lives out God's word or others' affirmation. Some stories are worth keeping.

Look back at the negative incident you have described. Whatever its source, are you living out of a belief in an untrue story about who you are called to be? You may have come to assign yourself a limiting script in life, such as, 'I will never be up to the mark'; 'I must never disappoint anybody'; 'I have to be wealthy to be happy'.

In the story of *Groundhog Day* the hero remained trapped in re-runs of the same 24 hours until he changed his behaviour for the better – living a different story within the same situation somehow released the calendar to move on. We might look for a similar new chapter in our own stuck places.

- Rewrite the second incident as if you were being shaped by God's story for you. If you find it easier, you could rewrite it replacing yourself with Jesus as a main character, to help you explore 'What Would Jesus Do?' in your situation and where it would take you.

- Write about how this changes your outlook and actions. Can you prayerfully place yourself into God's story in your decisions in this everyday situation, especially when faced with the temptation to relive an old, outdated story?

More things to try

1 Write your earthly story's outcome by writing your own obituary, as if written by someone else. How would you wish your life to be seen and celebrated by others? What legacy would you want to leave on earth, as a Christian? As you reread what you have written, consider how this might direct how you spend your time and energies now, and whether you need to make any adjustments.

2 There is a vogue for 'flash fiction' – the *very* short story – in our fast-paced age of internet, text and Twitter. The term was supposedly coined in 1992 for an anthology of very short stories. Definitions of 'very short' vary from around 1,000 words down to 150 and below. Ernest Hemingway famously won a bet that he could write a story in six words with 'For sale. Baby shoes. Never worn.' Reduce what you have written for the 'Telling our story: interactions' exercise above down to 300 words. This may mean focusing on just one section of the story, but it must work as a story. You now have a two-minute testimony. Are you willing to offer it in an appropriate two minutes?

3 Which Bible story has had a strong impact on you? Write it out in as much detail as you can from memory. Now go back to the Bible text. Compare what you have written with the original. Have you left out or emphasized anything different? What might that say about what this story means to you? Have you remembered the most important elements? How has the story shaped you? What do you understand it to be about? As you remind yourself of what you had forgotten, are there new things about this story you want to take on board? Write your reflections on this.

4 We form our own stories about other people, based on our immediate perceptions or others' opinions. These then become how we habitually see them. Sometimes we can be surprised

when people do something different from our 'script' for them. Write about a time when someone you thought you knew acted in a way you did not expect. What surprised you, and how did it alter what you had assumed and believed about that person? Where did your 'story' of that person come from – your own assumptions or others' tales? What do you believe now? How can we ensure we do not construct – and even tell – false stories about others?

6

Dialogue

———◆———

Graham did not expect to be conversing with a panda during his morning quiet time.

A dedicated and energetic vicar in an urban parish, he felt that his passion for growing God's kingdom sometimes met with apathy from the church and even within himself.

He agreed to engage this obstacle by writing a dialogue with it. Since it is easier to talk with something living, I suggested Graham envisage apathy as a person or animal. Graham saw it as a panda chewing on a bamboo shoot. He started writing.

'You're half-asleep. Get up!' Graham wrote. He was surprised by what he put down as the panda's reply: 'I'm not moving. I'm happy, but look at you! You're all agitated and frustrated. I'm attractive. People prefer me to you.'

Graham felt the panda was far too content with how things were. 'I wrote, "I may be future-focused but I've got a future. You're parasitical. Your life depends on others. You look content, but if you can't be bothered to breed and grow some bamboo for yourself, you'll die out."' As Graham continued, insights surfaced:

I realized that my driven-ness could be counterproductive in motivating the panda, and that I could learn something from it about contentment. I need a better balance between being committed to the kingdom to come, but able to rejoice in things now. I found myself praying about why I can be so driven.

If I'd just thought about apathy as an abstract concept, I'd have had more ideas, but I might have lost those key points. I may just have a few more chats with that panda.

Introducing dialogue

Our last chapter focused on storytelling. Dialogue between characters is one component of this, and its chief one when the story is presented as an on-stage drama: a play's dialogue propels the action as characters reveal or withhold information, act and react in relationship to each other, form alliances or have arguments, challenge or negotiate. As different voices interact, they also impact each other and stimulate shifts of perspective – as with Graham and the panda. Dramatic dialogue forms a bridge to a new place.

Although dialogue may be an unfamiliar writing format for us, it can be a helpful tool in writing our faith journey and moving us on. Dialogue is always written in the present tense – this gives it the capacity to make an encounter or experience alive in the here and now. This chapter will suggest ways of using dialogue to grow in our lives with God, our relationships with others and with aspects of ourselves, starting with Bible-based dialogues.

Dialogue in the Bible

Dialogue is part of the biblical drama. The theologian N. T. Wright describes the Bible as a five-act play: God's Creation; Man's Fall; Israel's story; Jesus' ministry; the Church's inception and growth. This last, unfinished act involves us as members of Christ's Church, anticipating his return. Within this drama, Wright asserts, Christians, who know the play's author and have received his Spirit, are called to play their parts, improvising their lines in accordance with the story's overall outcome.[1]

Most of the book of Job is in dialogue form, between Job and his so-called comforters and ultimately between God and Job himself. Scripture presents God as in direct dialogue with his people at various times: with Adam in the Garden of Eden (Genesis 3.8–13); Moses from a burning bush and face to face (Exodus 3, 4.1–16); with Elijah, cowering in a cave (1 Kings 19.1–18).

The Gospels record Jesus' many dialogues with those he encountered during his earthly life: his followers, friends, enemies and those seeking God or their personal healing. At times the drama of Jesus' interactions with others was enhanced by his silence (John 8.1–11). Dramatic dialogues also occur between Bible characters at key moments of action: Saul and David; Peter and Paul; Paul and his opponents.

Writing Bible-based dialogues

Using dialogue related to Scripture can help us approach God's word with both observation and intuition, and lift it to life from the page in a new way. We read the text carefully for information, and then engage our imagination.

In the New Testament, Jesus' followers have conversations significant enough to be referred to, even though they are not actually presented in the biblical text. You could explore writing the missing conversations between:

- Andrew and Simon Peter as Andrew tells him about Christ (John 1.40);
- a disciple and a father bringing his baby for Jesus to touch (Luke 18.15);
- the disciples as they argue about who is the greatest among them (Luke 9.46);
- Mary Magdalene and the disciples as she brings news of Jesus' resurrection (John 20.18);
- the newly converted Saul and the other disciples in Damascus (Acts 9.19);
- Saul and Barnabas as Barnabas seeks to bring Saul to Antioch (Acts 11.25);
- Paul and Barnabas as they argue (Acts 15.36–40).

As you start:

- Read around the relevant verses of your chosen dialogue, to be clear about what issue prompted it and what was its outcome. This will frame your writing.
- Glean what you can from the Bible to establish your speakers' situation, outlook, character and attitudes to each other.

- Supplement this with your own empathy – put yourself in your characters' sandals and try to imagine how they feel.
- Set your dialogue out as a play, with each speaker's name in the margin. Your dialogue need not involve long speeches.

You may prefer to deepen your understanding of biblical characters by participating in the dialogue in interviews with them. Choose a character who engages your interest – you may be drawn to that character as a person whose actions you find puzzling or inspiring, whose faith challenging or intriguing. Possible interviewees could include:

- Abraham after Isaac's birth (Genesis 21.1–5);
- Jacob after his marriage to Leah (Genesis 29.16–25);
- Gideon in battle (Judges 6.33—7.7);
- Esther after King Xerxes had made her his Queen (Esther 2);
- Jeremiah after his time in prison and in a cistern (Jeremiah 37—38);
- a person whom Jesus healed;
- Simon Peter;
- Judas.

As before, start by reading the character's story or the episode you want to explore for ideas about what to ask. What challenging questions would you put to your character if you dared? Now is your chance to go back in time as a no-holds-barred investigative journalist and find out what you've always wanted to know.

Interviewing a character in this way can deepen your understanding of his or her human situation, feelings, perspective and motives. You may find that as you are open to insight, the Holy Spirit's wisdom will supply answers beyond your own thinking.

Finally, you could go a step further and dispense with dialogue in favour of a straight monologue, writing a dramatic speech solely for your chosen character. This will challenge you to get right under this person's skin and feel as she or he felt.

Dialogue in prayer

We often speak of prayer as two-way communication, but if you are anything like me, prayers can easily drift into a monologue – or even a catalogue – of needs and concerns. Putting prayer to the page in the form of a written dialogue may help to address this. Writing our prayers can help us be more attentive. As we lift our pen to pause and listen, we make space in ourselves and on the page for God's response.

Quieten yourself for this conversation by calling to mind a setting that personally holds a sense of Jesus' presence for you – a special, quiet place outdoors or inside. Take some moments to enter this place in your mind's eye and settle in it. In your imagination, see Jesus approaching you. Notice what he looks like and what he is wearing. How will you both position yourselves for this conversation?

Open the dialogue by writing your words. When you have completed what you want to say, pause and write down whatever words surface as Jesus' response, trusting the Holy Spirit to keep you on track. If there is silence, note that too. When you sense the conversation coming to a natural end, conclude as you and Jesus take leave of one another. Gently return yourself to your everyday surroundings.

Reread this dialogue to prompt further prayer as you weigh what you sense Jesus' words to you were, in the light of Scripture and your current circumstances.

Dialogue with obstacles

The exercise above fostered direct, interactive prayer. But we may also use dialogue to help us be open to God's guidance and insight from another angle.

We often face obstacles on our journey of faith. These challenge our resources, energy and discernment. Is an obstacle a means by which God is guiding us to go another route, as it was with the circumstances that diverted Paul's missionary journey (Acts 16.6–8)? Is it a block that calls for faith, persistence and imagination to overcome, as with the men lowering their paralysed friend through the roof, for Jesus to heal (Mark 2.4)? By writing a dialogue with our obstacle, as Graham did with apathy, we may discern more of what is going on and how God is calling us to engage it.

Just as Graham gave apathy the form of a panda, you may wish to imagine your block (if it is not a person) as a living character – human or animal. For example, what do you imagine that sorrow, fear, rejection, a particular circumstance would look like? How would they talk?

Commit your dialogue-writing to God, asking the Holy Spirit to flood it with wisdom and knowledge. Write in an attitude of listening and willingness to engage with this obstacle, however you feel about it. In your written dialogue you might:

- express how you feel about the obstacle, and listen to how it feels about you;
- ask it what you might learn from its presence;
- allow it to talk about what it's doing;
- explore how you can best engage with it – Accept it? Work around it? Challenge it? Confront it? Allow it to redirect you?
- end when you feel clearer about the relationship you are to have with it.

Dialogue with God's silence

How can you dialogue when the other is silent? Elijah's experience in the Sinai cave was that God's presence was not in the noise of earthquake, wind or fire, but in 'the sound of sheer silence' (1 Kings 19.11–13). A dialogue exercise of faith-writing may foster your capacity to engage with God in his silence and express your willingness to make space for him.

Write as you want to pray to God at this moment, and then pause. You may wish to set a timer function on your watch or phone to discipline yourself to stay with the silence for a set period of, say, one minute or several, depending on how far you feel able to extend it. During this silence, do not try to think of things to write or say, or even what you think God might be saying. Seek to listen *to* the silence, not *through* it. Focus on your breathing if that helps.

After the set time, write as a prayer again for a few lines, and then leave another silent space. Continue until you can be settled with the conversational silence, and perhaps a little beyond that point.

Initially this exercise may feel a little strange – after all, nothing is happening. But a lot may be going on. For me, the process of writing prayer and pausing gradually settles my mind and focuses my attention. After a time, a restful sense of God's presence can emerge, rather like sitting with a friend and knowing you do not have to talk to enjoy one another's company. On good days I can remain in this settled state of being, and sense more clearly God's leading and direction amid the activities of the day. This does not happen every time, but it's well worth it when it does.

Difficult conversations

As well as reconnecting us in a more two-way communication with God, written dialogue may also help renew our relationship with another person, where something needs to change. That something may be addressing an issue, such as resolving a conflict or facing a problem. It may be within the relationship itself: we find the person difficult or feel stuck in an unhealthy and/or unloving pattern of relating.

Writing a dialogue with a difficult person or one with whom there is a difficulty can enable us to:

- dissipate our feelings about any conflict without harm or hurt to another;
- stop our anger or anxiety going around fruitlessly in our heads;
- clarify the real issues;
- identify the patterns of relating – or particular responses – we fear;
- prepare for that necessary but potentially hard conversation;
- open up some insight into the other person's point of view;
- break the deadlock;
- foster a more Jesus-centred perspective.

Prepare to write your dialogue with the difficult person or the difficulty by settling yourself in God's presence and the imagined presence of the other person.

If the issue for you is a difficult but necessary conversation, start your dialogue by writing what you want to say to raise the subject. Write the other person's reply. This may be your feared response, but now you have time to reflect on how you would reply if that was said. And what would the other person say next?

Try to keep writing until you and the other person have resolved the issue in your dialogue. You may find yourself refining and adjusting your words or approach as you go. Afterwards you may find you understand the issue and the other person's point of view better, and can address things face to face more calmly and constructively.

When I last tried this exercise myself I did not end up with a nice, neat dialogue. I was anxious about an upcoming difficult phone conversation. A counselling client had been lax about attending appointments, and the agency for whom I was working instructed me to close the contract. Nervous about the call, I jotted down how I would put this news, followed by my client's anticipated reaction.

So far so good. But reading this over, I wanted to rephrase my news. I crossed out my opening and squeezed in a rewrite above it. I also wanted to rework my response to her imagined reaction. This involved my checking her attendance on other dates. I scribbled this information in the margin. Then I found a question surfacing for myself. I drew a long, loopy line down the page, arrowed it and wrote: 'Why so anxious?' Even in writing this, I knew the answer: I'd mixed up the time of one particular appointment with my client, which made me reluctant to call her to account.

By now the page looked a mess, but inside my head things were much clearer. I made the call – to find her phone switched off, with no message-leaving facility. After all that, I ended up having to text the news! She did not call back.

In life, as in writing, things do not always go to plan, but the writing process did help me think through, gain insight and prepare for a task I was trying to avoid, however untidy the result on the page.

If your difficulty is more of a personality clash or a pattern of relating that is not positive or fruitful, determine at your dialogue's outset that you intend to find a constructive way to improve your communication and relationship. Expressing this could form your dialogue's opening words. How does the other person respond? Tell that person how you really feel, but also ask questions to understand his or her feelings as well. How do you come across? Try to see the relationship through the other's eyes and seek to 'hear' the answers that might be given. This exercise may help you see the other's perspective in a way that could shift your attitude.

If you find your dialogue becomes stuck, you could bring Jesus in to join the conversation. How does he see the situation? What would he say to each of you, and how do you both respond? As you become able to resume your original dialogue, you may wish to let Jesus leave. Do you talk to one another differently now? Is there any change you want to take from this exercise into your real relationship, to help move it towards being more loving and positive?

Dialogue recalled

Recalling an actual dialogue, rather than creating one, may highlight an area for growth, as Andrea found during her training for ordination. 'We were asked to write out an important conversation,' she told me, 'remembering it as best we could and including any significant actions or behaviour as "stage directions".' Andrea was surprised at how much she recalled of one particularly difficult conversation.

Andrea's elderly mother had died the week after Andrea left the area for theological college. Some weeks later, her friends Steve and Lucy visited. Not long before, Steve's father had nearly died after heart failure but had come through. Andrea recorded Steve's words about his father's amazing recovery: 'It was prayer that did it, I'm convinced. All that prayer – the whole church was praying.'

Andrea notes that she looked down at the table, uncomfortable: 'The church was praying for my mother too. Your father must have really wanted to live. He must have been fighting for his life.' 'He was fighting very hard,' said Steve, 'but it was prayer that made the difference. I'm sure of that.'

Andrea had struggled with this conversation. Why had Steve's father lived but her mother died, despite all her prayers? In a written reflection after this dialogue, she explored how Steve's words had touched a raw nerve in her grieving.

> This writing helped me face my mother's death. It was like a prayer, exploring where God was in it all, and coming to terms with being left by a remaining parent. I thought about what Steve was trying to say that I didn't hear, because I'd switched off into my own world. I hope I'd listen better if that sort of situation happened again.

Andrea identified a further inner conflict:

> When my mother spoke about her death, I didn't argue with her. I realized that there were two responses going on inside me. I spoke to her with the voice of acceptance and sub-mission, as in the hymn 'Abide with me'. But another voice inside was raging against death like the poet Dylan Thomas urging 'Do not go gentle into that good night'. Should I have responded to my mother with that voice?
>
> My written reflection became an inner dialogue between the 'Abide with me' versus the 'Do not go gentle' part of me! In the end I felt I'd responded to my mother appropriately. It was her time, even if it was not Steve's father's. Only God knows our timings.

Talking to ourselves

People sometimes worry that they are showing signs of madness if they are talking to themselves, yet most of us know the experience of having an inner dialogue going on in our heads. Dancing around our core ego and the voice of the Holy Spirit, different aspects of ourselves clamour for their say.

These aspects may be triggered by different situations and expect-ations. We might recognize them. Perhaps, as with Andrea's 'Abide with me' versus 'Do not go gentle' voices, we could even put labels on some conflicted elements – dutiful carer versus rebellious child; superhero versus self-pitying victim; free spirit versus disciplin-arian – although we are not necessarily comfortable with them.

Our goal as Christians is to become the complete, whole people we have been created to be, so our journey will involve healing and integrating these various aspects of ourselves.

Neither allowing these elements to drive our actions nor trying to crush them out of existence will help. We need to engage them. Since God loves every part of us unconditionally, we can accept that redemption on their behalf and seek to integrate them under Christ's lordship, allowing them to make their contribution to our whole personality.

One way to encourage this process is to write a dialogue. Choose an aspect of yourself that sometimes seems to have a life of its own. What is its key characteristic? Can you name or label this voice? Write a dialogue between you and this aspect of yourself to facilitate a two-way communication. Ensure that you:

- ask what prompts them to show up in your life;
- ask them how they are helping you;
- ask them what they need from you;
- let them know how you feel about them;
- find out how they feel about you;
- ask them what they are trying to teach you;
- explore how you can work together, with you in charge.

You may prefer to take a pair of contradictory sides of you, giving each side a voice to talk to the other and resolve their differences.

Dialogues can even be written with parts of the body, especially ones that are giving you pain. If you could give that aching back a voice, what would it say to you in response to the questions highlighted above? As whole people, we are created body, mind and spirit. Just as we listen to God, we need to listen to ourselves. The Holy Spirit may even be speaking to us through our bodies, if our minds are unreceptive.

And finally . . .

When I introduced a dialogue at a faith-writing workshop, with the idea that we might talk with different aspects of ourselves, it reminded Lesley of a letter she had written on the eve of her wedding. Although not set out in dialogue form, Lesley told me that she saw her piece as one part of herself talking to another.

> I wrote it from Miss Ashton, my single self, to Mrs Cunningham, the married self I was going to become the next day. It's one of the most significant letters I've ever written.
>
> I was frightened that as soon as I got into marriage, I'd forget the hard bits of being single, so I told my married self to remember the feeling of going home to a cold, empty flat, and what it was like when you were working late, with no one waiting for you back home.
>
> I offered advice on how my married self could remain sensitive and supportive, such as 'be willing to lend your husband to put up a curtain rail for a single woman'. I always used to worry what a wife might think if I asked a married man for practical help like this.
>
> For the sake of the singles that I knew, I didn't want my married self to forget these things.

While the present tense of a dialogue format brings an immediacy to any tension between the speakers, a letter can be an effective way of speaking to oneself at different points of time. Lesley has now been married 20 years. I have suggested she might like to write a reply to her single self, from the perspective of two decades as Mrs Cunningham.

More things to try

1 Write a prayer-dialogue with Jesus that starts with one of his questions in the 'Two-way questioning' section in Chapter 3, page 37. Picture yourself in the scene of the particular passage. Open the dialogue with Jesus putting the question to you.

2 The Old Testament is rich in incidents when God spoke with one of his people to call that person into his service or covenant – Abraham (Genesis 15), Samuel (1 Samuel 3), Isaiah (Isaiah 6), Jeremiah (Jeremiah 1). Write a dialogue that explores God's call on your life, either in the past or in the present if you think God is calling you to do something now.

7

Poetic writing 1

Rachel paused, reflecting on my question. We were sitting in a quiet, wood-panelled side room in Manchester Cathedral, away from the sunshine and bustle of city life. I had just asked this Anglican priest and Resident Cathedral Poet where her poetry writing had begun.

Rachel Mann started out as an academic philosopher and atheist. Surprised by a growing desire to pray, she ended up 'falling in love with God'. By her mid-twenties she was working on a Salford council estate and pursuing ordination. But in 1998 she was rushed to hospital as a medical emergency. A diagnosis of Crohn's disease was followed by a colostomy and a period of illness that left her unable to work for two years.

Rachel found her energetic and independent-spirited self draining away into depression:

> I faced issues of identity. Who was I now? Intellectually, I knew it wasn't the case, but emotionally it felt as though God was punishing me. My images of God fell apart. I could no longer believe in the God I used to believe in.

At this point, writing became a support: 'I needed to find my voice. I reached for words, and the words that became available to me had the feeling of poetry. Through them, I explored the interface between who God is and who I was.' Now a published poet, Rachel regards this early writing as 'not great poetry', but the process was very much a part of her faith journey.[1]

Coming to terms with powerful experiences can start with finding ways to name our response. As we search for words to express thoughts and feelings that arise from being out of our depth in unfamiliar territory, we may push into fresh ways of writing. Shaping these things with words helps us contain their intensity so they no longer overwhelm and incapacitate us.

Gillie Bolton comments that 'poetry seems to be a particularly therapeutic medium', adding that 'people who don't habitually write often turn to the poetic form when in trauma or emotional disturbance'.[2] The feelings that evoke poetic writing are not always negative emotions in the wake of a crisis. Our wider emotional life has a particular resonance with this genre.

In our spiritual life, we may also find we turn more naturally towards poetic writing to encapsulate something real but beyond the reach of our ordinary senses. Rowan Williams has spoken of poetry as finding 'new words for God'. As we are all uniquely made in God's image, we each have a capacity to combine words to express aspects of our faith in an individual way.

Poetry, however, can embrace all aspects of life across the spectrum, from the momentous to the ordinary. The poet and educator Jan Dean says, 'People sometimes have fixed ideas that poetry should have a certain form, content and appropriate subject, but it can focus on the most domestic of subjects. Poetry can be wonderful in celebrating and commemorating the small things.'[3]

While poetry may be inspired by anything from the death of a monarch to filling a kettle, the thought of it can evoke a sense of unease. Uncomfortable memories of schooldays, where poetry was a code to crack, writing to be deciphered rather than encountered, might have put you off reading it, let alone trying to write it. But you do not have to be a budding poet to use aspects of poetic writing fruitfully on your Christian journey. You may want to explore poetic language to:

- find words for a new, special or extraordinary experience;
- express emotions;
- enjoy using the music of words;
- enjoy shaping patterns of words;
- look for fresh connections and meanings;
- celebrate the wonder of an ordinary moment, object or activity;

- explore something familiar from a different angle;
- mine the depths and richness you discover when you are fully attentive.

In this chapter we will consider some biblical and Christian poetic writing; identify some of its key components; begin to explore them for ourselves.

Biblical poetic writing and beyond

However daunted we may feel at the thought of poetry, if we have read the Bible we are already readers of poetry and poetic writing.

The Old Testament contains several poetic books, such as Psalms, the Song of Solomon and Ecclesiastes. It also has a significant proportion of poetic writing across its canon. There are songs: Moses praises God for his people's deliverance through the parted Red Sea (Exodus 15.1–18); Hannah worships the Lord at the dedication of her God-given son, Samuel (1 Samuel 2.1–10); King David laments his friend Jonathan's death (2 Samuel 1.19–27).

In the New Testament, Luke's Gospel account of Christ's incarnation is surrounded with poetry. There is the Song of Mary, the Magnificat, proclaimed as she carries the unborn Christ (Luke 1.46–55); the Song of Zechariah, the Benedictus, at the birth of his son, John the Baptist (Luke 1.68–79); the Song of Simeon, the Nunc Dimittis, at the infant Christ's dedication in the Temple (Luke 2.29–32).

Christians of every generation have turned to poetry and song to express their faith. One of our earliest English Christian poems, the eighth-century *The Dream of the Rood*, evokes Christ's death and resurrection from the perspective of the cross. Abundant and diverse Christian poetry since then includes the intensity of the seventeenth-century Anglican priest John Donne's cry, 'Batter my heart, three-personed God'; the musical inventiveness of Gerard Manley Hopkins' praise to the God of 'dappled things'; the metrical formality of Christina Rossetti's 'In the bleak midwinter', written in the Victorian era. The twentieth century brought the reflective

insight of T. S. Eliot into the paradox of birth and death in the
'Journey of the Magi', as well as the uncompromising honesty of
R. S. Thomas, drawn to pray to:

> ... this great absence
> that is like a presence ...[4]

Faith, writing and poetry did not always go together for the Jesuit
priest Gerard Manley Hopkins. He gave up writing poetry for Lent
in 1866. Two years later, aged 24, he put all his poetry on a bonfire
and stopped writing it altogether, worried that it would distract
rather than enhance his religious life.

In 1875 Hopkins saw a newspaper article on a shipwreck in the
North Sea. The fatalities included five German nuns. His superior
observed that someone should write a memorial about this.
Encouraged that his poetic gift could now be integrated with his
religious calling, Hopkins wrote 'The Wreck of the Deutschland',
his first poem for seven years. He continued to write, but shunned
publication, concerned for its dangers of self-centredness. He died
in 1889, his poetry ultimately published via his friends in 1918.

Elements of poetic writing

If you struggle to define poetry, you are not alone. Poets themselves
come at the issue from various angles. Samuel Taylor Coleridge
saw poetry as 'the best words in the best order'. For Thomas Hardy
it was 'Emotion put into measure'.

Despite the lack of one catch-all definition, we may highlight
some of poetry's essential qualities as:

- attentiveness to an object, experience, event or feeling that
  engages us;
- selectivity and focus in our choice of words;
- shaping of words into a form or structure;
- sensitivity to the music of words – their sound or rhythm pattern;
- inclusion of images or figurative language.

Here we will focus on attentiveness and issues of selection, structure
and pattern.

When writing poetry, I start by gathering material. It's vital to pay full attention and write down what I'm really experiencing. Once I've something written down, I look for the word or phrase where the energy lies. There's real prayer in the attention that comes first, but rewriting and shaping the poem is as important spiritually. The Holy Spirit can inspire all stages. The process of working with a poem can be as important as the end result. Later I find that in what I've written, something speaks to me and I know more about the world and my life than before.

Andrew R.

Writing attentively

For my friend Christine, writing poetry is the challenge to 'say something difficult to express in as many words as necessary but as few as possible'. This distilling into words of a particular experience, emotion, insight, event or subject requires deep and focused attention.

Being attentive is not just a key component of creative writing. The fifteenth-century French priest and philosopher Nicolas Malebranche wrote that 'attentiveness is the natural prayer of the soul'. So practising attentiveness in poetic writing might help us on our way to a deeper stillness that enriches our prayer life as well.

As an exercise, set up your writing materials at home – pen, paper and sticky notes – and then go out for a walk. Set a leisurely pace, breathe deeply and take time to stop and stare. Take things slowly, allowing yourself to notice what is around you. Really look at your surroundings and consciously absorb and examine what you see. Find something to bring back home with you, or take a photograph of something to bring back instead.

Back home, explore your object (or look at your photograph). If you have the object with you, feel and smell it as well as look at it. Pay it close attention, looking at it as if you had never seen it before. Now write down exactly what you notice. Your writing may start quite factually but become more colourful and inventive as you stay with the process. We can become aware of the strangeness and wonder of even the most ordinary things the longer we focus on them. Allow your imagination to play with any associations and possibilities your object evokes, and write them down.

Once you have taken this stage as far as you can, read over the fragments you have collected. Choose the ones that most appeal to you, for whatever reason, and write each one on a separate sticky note. Now experiment with ordering them by moving the sticky notes around to create different sequences, perhaps arranging them on a table or wall. Choose the order you find most pleasing. Do not worry about how 'good' a poem results. You have engaged in the attentiveness, selection and arrangement of words at the heart of the poetic process.

If you prefer, you could do this exercise with a photograph or picture that appeals to you, perhaps from a magazine such as the *National Geographic* or a newspaper colour supplement.

Afterwards, reflect on your experience of the exercise, perhaps writing down your thoughts. What might this attentive approach have to offer to how you pray? What might it have to offer to the way you go through an ordinary day?

One of the great British television interviews of the late twentieth century was with Dennis Potter, who was dying of cancer. The writer told the interviewer, Melvyn Bragg, that he had discovered the intensity of life in the present tense. No longer was the plum-tree blossom outside his window merely 'nice blossom'. He now saw it as 'the whitest, frothiest, blossomest blossom that there ever could be . . . The nowness of everything is absolutely wondrous.'

Being attentive to the present moment helps us notice what can otherwise be missed. As the Christian leader Rob Bell commented, a piece of writing often works because it prompts a sense of recognition: we realize the truth of what is being described, because we half-saw it as we hurried past. Only the writer was going slowly enough to notice it properly, pay attention and write it down. If we walked through each day with the patience, attention and imagination we applied to this exercise, we might taste more of the abundant life God has given us.

Poetry is a tool for understanding – recollecting and exploring feelings about what has happened, although not in the intensity of emotion at the time. A poem has to be the best poem I can make. I want to connect up words' meanings, sounds and the pictures they create.

I start by writing things down, just talking on to paper. Then I work on these fragments – pare them down, order them in a pleasing way. Often, when I come back to the writing later, other insights come up.

A lot of the process is listening. I know what something is like but I haven't got the words for it. I wait for them to rise up. Sometimes it feels as though they are given. At other times it's like getting blood from a stone.   *Jan*

Forms and shapes

Placing your sticky-note words and phrases in different arrangements in the last exercise was a way of putting them in a deliberate order. You were beginning to think about your writing's form.

While prose is poured on to the page in a continuous stream, poetic writing is more deliberately shaped. There are many ways to order our words poetically. The first feature that springs to mind for many of us when we think about poetry is regular rhyming lines, spoken in a sing-song rhythm.

Shaping words into separate lines or verses and creating patterns of sound are two aspects of forming poetry, but there are others. Hebrew poetry's most common device patterned sense rather than sound. This is called parallelism. In this verse from Amos (5.24), 'let justice roll down like waters, and righteousness like an ever-flowing stream', the second statement, after the comma, 'parallels' the first. It uses the same structure and echoes its meaning, to underline it for emphasis. Proverbs 10.1 uses the parallel structure differently. In 'A wise child makes a glad father, but a foolish child is a mother's grief', the structure of the first statement is repeated but the second one has a contrasting meaning. Both verses are shaped around a sequence of thought.

Using simple forms

Part of the challenge and satisfaction in poetic writing is finding a form to express our experience. We have already noted how God brings shape to the void as he forms his Creation in Genesis 1. As we experience the stuff of life outside or discover emotions and insights rising up inside, giving them a form can help us both contain and articulate them to ourselves, God and perhaps others.

Using a form also means exercising our God-given capacity to select what we include. This discipline can help us reflect on how we make choices in other areas of life. Do we find it hard to focus and identify our priorities in what we do? What we buy? Where we commit? If we try to do everything in life we end up accomplishing nothing. In our writing, too, we need to make choices if we are not to miss seeing the wood for the trees.

Creativity involves imagination and possibilities alongside decision-making and selection – of what to leave out as well as what to put in. Poetic writing illustrates this perhaps more intensely than other writing genres: the wordless white space on the page contributes to its effect. Do we leave space in our lives too?

One straightforward form to start with is a list poem. You may wish to use some list material you have already written from Chapter 3. A list poem can be as simple or sophisticated as you like. It can be particularly satisfying to use a repeated refrain, to give the piece a greater unity of form. Try composing a thanksgiving list poem by beginning every new line with 'Thank you Lord, for . . .'.

A repeated phrase or refrain, interwoven between different lines, can also work well. This combines the familiar with the fresh. The psalms, being songs, sometimes include refrains, such as 'his stead-fast love endures for ever' (Psalm 136) and 'Praise him in', 'Praise him for', through to 'Praise him with' (Psalm 150). You could experiment with using these refrains within your own praise poem.

You could also go one step further to create your own refrain, choosing a repeated form of words and a set number of lines per verse of your poem. Sue Mayfield, a writer and writing prac-titioner, finds it helpful to look for a refrain as a 'hook' for a poem as she generates ideas.[5] The poem below, 'Gifts of the Christ Child', began with her exploring the question, on a pre-Christmas retreat day, 'What are the gifts that the Christ Child is bringing?' Look at how the repeated 'I give . . .' draws together the different gifts into her single, song-like poem:

> I give you words
> words that bridge spaces, open doors
> heal wounds, unfasten chains
> I, the word made flesh,
> give words to you.
>
> I give you tenderness
> skin that smarts, eyes that weep
> a heart that longs – loves, aches, breaks.
> I, the helpless child
> give tenderness to you.
>
> I give you flesh
> ordinariness and sense
> bread and touch, perfume and blood
> I give you earthiness divine
> I, Immanuel, give my flesh to you.
>
> I give you beauty
> colour and song
> light and laughter, wild delight
> the radiance of an old man's face
> I, whom angels worship
> give beauty to you.

Another accessible form of poem is an acrostic, where the first letter of each line forms a pattern, word or phrase when read downwards. The most basic acrostic is an alphabet poem, such as Psalm 119, in its original Hebrew, although there are other variations to try. For instance, you could write a prayer that follows phrases from the Lord's Prayer through the first letter of each line. The phrase 'Hallowed be thy name' could be the basis of an acrostic praise prayer-poem. Try 'Give us today our daily bread' to form the template for prayers of petition. 'Thy kingdom come; thy will be done' could be the start-point for an intercessory prayer-poem.

A set-form poem such as a cinquain can help us focus our attention and choose our words carefully. A cinquain is, as the name suggests, a five-line poem. Devised in the 1900s, it takes its inspiration from Eastern poetic forms such as the Japanese haiku. One cinquain format is:

Line 1: a one-word title;
Line 2: a two-word descriptive phrase or two adjectives;
Line 3: a three-word action phrase or three verbs – perhaps all ending in 'ing';
Line 4: a five-word phrase or sentence conveying a feeling connected to the title;
Line 5: a one-word summing-up or alternative synonym for the title.

Writing this very contained form can be satisfying and even a little addictive. When I asked Patricia to try her hand at a cinquain, she mailed me a page of them, including:

> Grandchildren.
> Special and beautiful,
> Challenging, playing, engaging.
> They bring such fun and laughter into our lives.
> Joy.

> Sunset,
> Glorious, colourful,
> Shining, sinking, disappearing,
> It gives light to the other side of the world.
> Nightfall.

> Football,
> Agony and ecstasy,
> Scoring, winning, losing,
> It is in your blood and part of your being.
> Everton.

You could write a cinquain on something precious or just noticed in passing: an everyday object or a pet. You could also intentionally address your attention to God in a devotional cinquain by choosing one of the names of Jesus as a title – Shepherd, King, Saviour, Son – and then listening quietly for words that emerge for the other lines. It can be fun to play with a cinquain by swapping the title-line, line 1, with the summing-up line, line 5, and seeing what effect this has on your poem.

As this writing engages our focused attention we may settle into a quieter, more prayerful frame of mind. In stillness we observe and reflect, open to receiving the words we need. Composing a cinquain can be one way of casting our anxieties on to God. We let go, allowing our creative poem-making to fill the space previously occupied by worries and fears. It may also help us foster patience. If we are waiting at a bus stop or in the doctor's surgery, we could use the time to look around for a suitable cinquain subject to work on.

Lastly, you may like to try a couple of simple forms that comprise short lines with set numbers of syllables (single units of sound) per line. These may contain fewer words, but be warned: this may make selecting just the right ones even more demanding.

The tetractys – based on an Ancient Greek mathematical figure – consists of five lines, starting with one syllable, increasing by one syllable per line, until a final jump to ten – the total of the first four lines combined – on the fifth line.

Line 1: one syllable;
Line 2: two syllables;
Line 3: three syllables;
Line 4: four syllables;
Line 5: ten syllables.

The poem's aim is to present a complete thought. Rosanne, who told me about the tetractys, read me one she had written to encapsulate the story of Noah. She entitled it 'Obedience':

> Flood?
> Build boat?
> Animals?
> Family, Lord?
> Perhaps you're kidding. I'll do your bidding.

Linda enjoys writing poetry in a form known as the piku. This is a three-line poem, also based on syllable count, as follows:

Line 1: three syllables;
Line 2: one syllable;
Line 3: four syllables.

The piku also has a mathematical origin. Its syllable count per line replicates the first three digits of pi – 3.14 – and its name is a combination of 'pi' and 'haiku', the latter being another three-line poetic form from Japan. The piku's sparse form focuses on a single idea. Linda[6] has written a series inspired by verses in 1 Corinthians 13, opening with verses 1–3:

> Talk is cheap:
> it's
> not love, it's noise.

> To know all,
> but
> not love? Useless.

> Charity
> starts
> with love, not cash.

If you find this mathematical aspect of poetry unappealing, we are about to change tack as we turn to poetic images in our next chapter.

More things to try

1 Experiment with the alphabet poem, the most basic form of the acrostic form. For example, try beginning each line with a refrain: 'Thank God that you are ...' and follow on with an aspect of God to praise – 'Almighty', 'Beautiful', 'Compassionate' and so on. You could also do this with things to thank God for.

This form could also be used to express the range of your responses to God: 'Lord, I adore you', 'I behold you', 'I confess to you' and so on – or vice versa to declare God's response to you: 'Lord, you affirm me', 'you befriend me', 'you care for me' and so on.

2 Use a refrain from Psalm 136 or 150 to create your own praise poem by alternating it with your own line. You could also choose any short Bible verse that is meaningful to you, to interweave with lines of personal prayer, or use the words of Jesus:

- 'Abide in my love' (John 15.9);
- 'My peace I give to you' (John 14.27);
- 'I am the way, and the truth, and the life' (John 14.6);
- 'Do not worry about your life' (Matthew 6.25);
- 'For God all things are possible' (Mark 10.27);
- 'I am with you always' (Matthew 28.20).

Or words from the Old Testament:

- 'The LORD is my strength and my might' (Exodus 15.2);
- 'There is no Rock like our God' (1 Samuel 2.2);
- 'You are a God ready to forgive, gracious and merciful' (Nehemiah 9.17);
- 'This is the day that the LORD has made' (Psalm 118.24);
- 'Do not fear, for I have redeemed you' (Isaiah 43.1);
- 'The sun of righteousness shall rise' (Malachi 4.2).

3 A poem is a work of art, with carefully selected content, shape and form. In the same way, each of us is a poem written by God. We have a unique physical shape and beauty, personality and gifts, opportunities and limitations. We respond to God within the framework he has formed for us. Reflect on what sort of poem you think you are. Do you have a regular rhythm, rhyme and form, or are you more a free-verse creation? Explore ways of describing yourself in poetic writing to express who you uniquely are. Play with images and phrases, rhymes and sound patterns, lines or arrangements of words on the page until you are satisfied with the fit.

4 If you found the previous activity challenging, try writing in the set form of the cinquain with yourself as the subject. Your material from the previous activity may suggest some content.

You could offer your poem to God as a way of giving yourself back to your maker. You may wish to share your writing with a trusted friend, or even write a cinquain about one another. How you encapsulate each other in this short, poetic form may help you see aspects of yourselves more clearly.

8

Poetic writing 2

———••●••———

> Turquoise skips like a happy child
> humming to itself.

This is the opening line of 'Turquoise', a poem Alis wrote for a writing workshop. Everyone chose a colour and answered questions about it to stimulate ideas for images (reproduced at the chapter's end to try for yourself, along with Alis' poem). Then they used this material to create list poems about their colour. Alis later described the impact of the exercise:

I picked turquoise because it's my favourite colour. Just thinking about it made me realize how happy it makes me feel. I worked through the questions, but once I started the poem, it took on a life of its own. The writing of it was quite a revelation. 'Skipping along like a happy child' just popped out spontaneously. A happy child is a carefree one, not beset by problems.

I struggle with depression, and after I wrote this poem, I decided to wear something in one shade or other of turquoise every day – a t-shirt or even just a pair of earrings or a scarf. When I'm out shopping, I've started looking around for turquoise things to wear!

Choosing to put on this colour is like choosing to have a positive approach. I remind myself that it's a happy colour. I'm making an effort to wear something to support my mood. It's very important to my well-being.

I love how words in poetry can hold layers of meaning and make people think about things in a different way.

In the last chapter we looked at two starting points for poetic writing: attentiveness and using a form. In this chapter we will explore a third one: the image.

Images in poetic writing

An image is a way of putting something hidden or abstract into a concrete shape or picture, just as Alis captured the mood of the colour turquoise through the image of the singing, skipping child. We may want to write things that are hard to put into words but that we sense are around at the edge of our consciousness. This can push us to find an image that somehow expresses it for us.

Images are the lifeblood of poetic writing. They do not itemize measurable facts but highlight something underlying – a truth, issue, feeling or connection. Images help open up what is otherwise inaccessible. In Alis' phrase, they 'hold layers of meaning', to explore and discover. Images can bypass our conscious calculating to create a highway to the heart.

Our everyday language is coloured by images in familiar expressions such as: 'You could cut the air with a knife'; 'She really gets under my skin'; 'He is as cunning as a fox'. Some images become so overworked as to be clichés, such as the rose to represent romantic love.

In describing something to someone not there to see it, we often resort to images, comparing it to something concrete that our hearers will recognize. We may say something is like something else – a simile, as in Jesus' words, 'The kingdom of heaven is like . . .' or that something *is* something else – a metaphor, as in Jesus' statement, 'I am the bread of life'.

Images for the spiritual in the Bible

Jesus' images are windows to help us see spiritual realities more nearly and understand them more clearly. In John's Gospel, Jesus uses images to illuminate himself and his relationship to his people: he is the bread, gate and good shepherd (6.35; 10.9, 11).

When Nicodemus approaches him, Jesus responds with an image, telling this seeker that those who desire to enter God's kingdom must be 'born again' (John 3.1–8). Matthew's Gospel records how Jesus also uses images to communicate God's kingdom itself, such as, 'The kingdom of heaven is like . . . a mustard seed . . . treasure hidden in a field . . . a wedding banquet' (Matthew 13.31, 44; 22.2).

Paul's letter to the Colossian Christians describes Jesus himself as an image – 'the image of the invisible God', whose coming as Emmanuel opens up a visible connection to the unseen God (Colossians 1.15). In Jesus' earthly life and redemptive work, we encounter God enfleshed rather than as a theological proposition.

The Bible's prophetic writings from Isaiah onwards draw richly on the vivid images of poetic language to reveal and communicate God's truths, events and their meanings beyond the reach of human discernment or understanding. Isaiah's prophecies of God's coming age when 'The wolf shall live with the lamb' (Isaiah 11.6) proclaim an era of peace so absolute that it can only be conveyed in images that bring together opposites irreconcilable in the natural world as we know it. Revelation, the Bible's final book, comprises colourful and complex images in prophetic visions given to John, forth-telling and foretelling the wider canvas of God's ultimate dealings with humankind.

Historical accounts and poetic imagery can both express truth, even if only the former is literal fact. The Bible uses both sorts of language. Christians may agree that God's word is true, but find differences surfacing when there is confusion about how to read a particular passage. Is God's truth being presented as literal fact or indicated through an image? Engaging God's word includes discerning the sort of language in which it is being communicated.

Re-imagining images from psalms

One way to explore images in writing our faith is to take Scripture passages where they are used and find ways to update or even personalize them. The Japanese poet Toki Miyashina famously reworked Psalm 23 as a 'Psalm for Busy People' in his modern city culture. He started by changing 'The Lord is my shepherd' to 'The Lord is my pace-setter'. You might try reworking David's words for yourself. Open with 'The Lord is my . . .', inserting your own equivalent of Shepherd, and continue through the psalm, rewriting it with images appropriate for your personal thanksgiving for God's provision.

You could re-imagine and update other psalms from their ancient, agricultural context to reflect the world of twenty-first-century town dwellers. For example:

- Psalm 29.3–11: look at the different illustrations of the power of the Lord's voice. What might be some modern equivalent images?
- Psalm 36.5–12: can you think of fresh images for God's unfailing love, righteousness, love and justice? Can you think of another image to convey his protection and provision?
- Psalm 37.1–7: look at images of the wicked and the good, and God's dealings with them. Can you update these?
- Psalm 42: look at the images of deer and the psalmist's memories of good times. What might replace the procession and the lands of Jordan and Hermon in contemporary or your personal experience?

The aim here is not to pull apart God's word but to use your image-making to come closer to its heart, understand its meaning and apply it more directly to life today. You might find yourself doing some Bible study to deepen your knowledge of what the psalms' images would have meant to those who first heard them. This could trigger your imagination in devising their equivalent.

Finding an image

'What does God's love look like to you?' Jan Dean, a poet and educator, was putting me on the spot over a cup of tea in her lounge. 'Think of something concrete', she insisted. 'It's like being a pea snuggled in a peapod', I found myself saying. 'And what does that actually feel like?' I was still not being let off the hook. 'I suppose, like being wrapped up tight in a duvet', I replied.

Jan was telling me how, for her, the key to starting a poem is finding a vivid image to bring substance and focus to our subject:

> As adults, we tend to think that abstraction is grown-up, but images are powerful. So if you're writing about loss, think of a real memory, object, place or activity that links you to the person. In your mind's eye, pan the camera in to focus on specific detail. Explore connections. Reflect on what this reminds you of. Now write about that, not the person.

Images of living in God's kingdom

We could apply this approach by exploring images of how we see ourselves living as Christians in God's kingdom. Try to find a concrete image in answer to any or all of the following:

- If God's kingdom was a kitchen, what would you be?
- If God's kingdom was a rainbow, what colour would you be?
- If God's kingdom was a garden, what flower would you be?
- If God's kingdom was a zoo, what animal would you be?
- If God's kingdom was a furniture shop, what would you be?

Be open to whatever images or ideas spring to mind in response to these questions, and write them straight down, however odd or disconnected it may seem to your critical mind.

Now choose an image and write it in the middle of a new page. Explore it by writing around it any links, associations or connections the image has for you. What does it make you think of? Be open to new insights surfacing. Are you at ease with this image or would you rather be something else? If so, what?

You could now order some or all of these fragments as you wish, separating them into lines or grouping them into verses. More things may come up for you as you reflect on your words and shape them. Doing this can be an offering yourself to God to use as he will in his kingdom, or form a more questioning prayer if you feel a disconnect between the image you chose and the one you long to be.

The fruit of the Spirit

Another resource for looking at ways of linking abstract truth to a concrete image to help it live more vividly is the fruit of the Spirit: 'love, joy, peace, patience, kindness, generosity, faithfulness, gentleness, and self-control' (Galatians 5.22–23).

Choose one fruit to focus on, perhaps one you sense is at your growing edge. Use your imagination and pen to explore the questions below – they are there to prompt you to make your fruit accessible via the senses. You may prefer to start by linking it to a specific, literal fruit. What does your Christ-charactered quality:

- look like?
- sound like?
- smell like?
- taste like?
- feel like to the touch?

Jot down your reflections as they arise:

- Can you think of an action, snapshot or scene to sum up your fruit?
- Which sense is easiest to link to an image?
- Which answer intrigues you most?
- What might this say about you and your chosen fruit?
- What insights or challenges arise from this material?

Your writing can be set aside to return to later and add to as new things emerge. You may wish to select what feels most significant, to shape and unify into one piece of poetry. You may want to leave out some images; add to others; find an order that feels right; decide on lines and verses; perhaps play with sound patterns such as rhyme or alliteration. You could write the words in different shapes on the page (in a spiral, columns or twisting lines); in capitals; in different colours. Enjoy the process, without worrying about the standard of the final product.

Letting the image find you

Poetic writing, as we have noted, has a particular resonance with our emotional life. The American poet Robert Frost asserted that, 'in a complete poem, the emotion has found its thought and the thought has found its words'.

So far we have started with something abstract and looked for a concrete image to express it. We may find an emotional connection released by starting the other way around: identifying an image outside ourselves and letting it 'speak' to us in whatever way emerges. This can be helpful in allowing what is significant to surface naturally, without us forcing the process. The image we are drawn to observe will touch whatever inner connection may be ripe for us to express or address at this particular time.

Psalm 1 uses the image of the tree as a picture of a person whose life is rooted in God and growing in righteousness. Using that idea, take a walk or look at photographs or pictures to find a tree that particularly appeals to you.

Mind-map your tree, taking time to notice and describe its trunk, leaves and branches:

- What species is it?
- What does it look, feel and smell like?
- How would you describe it?
- What is its age or season?

Branch out – no pun intended – using imagination alongside observation:

- What are your tree's roots like?
- How does it feel?
- Does it seem healthy – fruitful – neglected – pruned – treated – alone – damaged/scarred in some way?
- Where are you physically in relation to that tree?
- Where would you like to be?

You may find that your reflections on the tree begin to make connections with who and where you are in life just now. If you saw the tree as an image of your life, what would it highlight about your current state – emotional, spiritual, physical? You may wish to write your reflections into a shape on the page – perhaps even a tree shape.

Writing our emotions

Facing emotions head-on can be a raw experience. Coming at them via an image can make them accessible to us in a more gentle and approachable way. As one of my first counselling clients struggled to address some overwhelming feelings, we somehow stumbled on the language of images as a way of talking about them – from a candlelit cave to a breakthrough the client described as like a heavy obstruction lifted from a struggling waterwheel.

Three years ago my husband broke a glass – not an ordinary glass, but one of a wedding-gift set of four individually crafted wine glasses, bought at the hotel where we had had our wedding reception.

Let's just say my feelings about the breakage were complex. I was not sure that I could trust myself to express them calmly, so I went away to write. Rather than address the feeling directly, I started with the image of the broken glass and the incident that had led to it:

> 'It just broke in my hand.' He shrugs,
> holding two fragments of wine glass like wings,
> snapped off in a moment.
> Soapy water; hidden cutlery; broken glass.
> In another trice, all is thrown away,
> trashed with a clink in the bin.

I continued to focus on the glass, but to do so I needed to look more attentively at the three that remained. Each had an individual etching of a bird on it. What species of bird had been on the broken glass? I did not know. I realized I had not looked very carefully before, and began to wonder just how much I had really treasured this gift. My perspective began to shift unexpectedly beyond lamenting this loss, towards what became the last verse of the poem:

Perhaps things are bound to break –
The little fractures of our careless kitchen days;
Edges frayed but forgiven,
And now, a strange, re-completed set of four:
Three wine glasses.
And one poem.

I felt calmer and more able to talk about what had happened. The broken glass challenged me to accept this world's vulnerabilities and the need for forgiveness amid brokenness. The poem also became a permanent and unbreakable commemoration of the glass that had gone.

If you are nudged or unsettled by an emotional response to something, it may help to start by linking it to an image – perhaps from the incident that has triggered the emotion – as a starting point for exploration. Write about the image:

- What do you see in it?
- What associations does it have for you?
- What is it saying?

You may find that as you start to explore it, resolution comes by a route you did not expect.

More things to try

1 You could repeat the trees exercise outlined in this chapter, but this time focusing on a tree in the Bible. Possibilities include:

- the 'tree of the knowledge of good and evil' in the garden of Eden (Genesis 2.16–17);
- the unfruitful fig tree that Jesus cursed (Mark 11.12–14);
- the 'sycomore' tree that Zacchaeus climbed (Luke 19.4);
- the tree on which Jesus was crucified (Acts 5.30);
- the 'tree of life' in the new Jerusalem (Revelation 22.2);
- the vine as symbol of Israel (Isaiah 5.1–7);
- the evergreen cypress for God himself (Hosea 14.8);
- the olive tree for God's people (Romans 11.24).

Research your tree, in its biblical context and beyond. You may wish to find a picture of it. Jot down associations, feelings and images that spring to mind in connection with this tree. Walk around it in your mind's eye, 'become it', notice all you can about it. Imagine you are seeing it for the first time. What is it *really* like?

Jot down your responses and use your notes as a resource to select the words and phrases that most strike you. Experiment with arranging, adding to or shaping these words into a form you find meaningful and pleasing.

2 Images of God: list the different titles and images applied to Jesus – good shepherd, Prince of Peace, light of the world, door, vine and so on.

Choose the image you are most naturally drawn to and write it in the middle of the page. Now use your imagination and write around it any words or associations connected with that image that spring to mind. Reread what you have written, reflecting on what it is about this image that most engages you with God.

Now choose an image that you relate to less easily and go through the same process. What is it about this image that is more of a sticking point for you?

If you were to sum up in an image of your own who God is to you today, what would it be? What are the significant associations of that image for you? Can you link these to aspects of God as he makes himself known in Scripture?

3 Choose a colour that draws your attention, and use the following questions to generate some images:

- What mood is your colour?
- What do you associate with your colour?
- What place(s) does your colour take you?
- How does your colour move?
- In what season was your colour born?
- What time of day or night does it look like?
- What does your colour sound, smell or taste like?
- What does your colour wish for?

- What is your colour a box of?
- What is your colour a song of?
- What is your colour a shape of?
- Who are your colour's friends?

Select, say, six answers to arrange into a list poem, as Alis did for her poem, 'Turquoise', below.

> Turquoise skips like a happy child
> humming to itself.
>
> Turquoise is a chameleon colour
> born of a blue-green marriage.
>
> Turquoise delights in very existence
> dances with the knowledge that no eye
> perceives it the same.
>
> Turquoise is the colour of water and movement
> not land or solidity.
>
> Turquoise will not be defined or restrained.
> It will trickle through your fingers
> like warm sand.
>
> Turquoise sparkles in sunshine
> greets everyone with warm smiles
> and open arms.
>
> Turquoise is a hurrah colour,
> a box of treats, a song of joy.

9

Writing through loss towards healing

———◆●◆———

I stood with my friend Jenny in the half-light backstage. We listened to the audience's chatter, waiting for our cue to turn the heavy handle that pulled back the stage curtains. Our task for this school play was a nerve-wracking responsibility for two second-formers. The drama, written by our English teacher, celebrated the life and times of our girls' grammar school in its 50th year. Frequent scene-changes meant that we curtain operators had to be on our toes.

My favourite scene comprised poems written by pupils, read to music. One began, 'Someone gave me a diary', which the speaker said she did not need to write down all the joys of her current romance. Many pages were left blank. Now, to her distress, the relationship was over. The poem's final words, 'No matter how many words I write or diaries I fill, only those empty pages will move me', sent a shiver down my spine every night.

Perhaps even then I identified with the tendency to turn to words when times were tough. The page was a safe space to express and explore adolescent struggles. When I was happy and active, I didn't want to interrupt life by writing about it.

You may also find yourself more drawn to pick up a pen in life's lows than its highs. When loss cuts across our life's flow, writing may help to:

- support us in lonely times;
- contain our turmoil in overwhelming times;
- explore our growing edges in challenging times;
- provide an anchor-point in changing times;
- bring order and clarity in confusing times;
- suggest a direction in uncertain times.

As we commit ourselves to being open on the page and in God's presence, we may find deeper possibilities for healing and growth beyond loss. In this chapter we will revisit some writing modes from Chapter 2, in the context of loss, and see how some Christians have used the written word as part of their restoration by the living Word.

Starting with feelings

Loss is experienced emotionally – in sadness, loneliness, fear, bewilderment, disorientation. We may feel fragile or numb, angry or despairing. Finding a way of expressing our feelings can start us moving through our loss. Writing them down can be particularly valuable where no one else is around to talk to.

Writing in a feeling mode can help us name and acknowledge our feelings honestly in God's presence. We sometimes say that strong emotions put us 'beside ourselves', strangers to the self we know. Writing helps us put the emotions on the outside, making them visible and less invasive. The page's white space becomes an image of God's pure, non-judgemental acceptance and containing safety.

We can flow-write our feelings in a spontaneous outpouring to discharge their energy. If our feelings are choked up, confused or even contradictory, we can just write in lists, fragments and phrases. The psalmist's question in Psalm 42, 'Why are you cast down, O my soul?' could be one to pose and answer. The verse could be written in the centre of the page, with words and phrases added around it.

There are two caveats to the expressive writing of feelings. Jane Moss, a writing practitioner, has found that, 'for the bereaved, this approach may be too blunt and directive. My observation is that few people wish to stare their grief in the face on the page; they live with it all the time and know it well.'[1]

The other addresses the issue of a workshop participant, who came wanting to know how to use writing to stimulate personal change: 'When I read through my journals,' she said, 'they're just a pouring out of angst.'

James Pennebaker's research, referred to in Chapter 1, has indicated that while the expressive writing of our emotions can be part of the healing process, it will not do the job alone. It needs to be linked to writing about the difficult events themselves. Louise De Salvo notes that the students who benefited from writing in Pennebaker's research had not only expressed their feelings on paper but also:

> reflected upon the significance of events, attaining insights into their traumas and achieving some distance from them. Through writing about events *and* feelings, students integrated the two; they understood what had occurred and how they felt about it, and they assimilated the meaning of this event into their lives.[2]

There needs to be movement on a journey. Even the psalmist's honest laying out of his feelings is only the starting point. By the end of a psalm, his position and outlook have shifted towards a more God-centred perspective, even if a resolution has not been fully reached.

When you have written your difficult feelings, take time to discern your next step in using this writing to move forward. Various possibilities may nurture a momentum of spiritual change. You could:

- shred your writing as part of a prayer of letting go to God;
- swap around your writing's list items, fragments or images into a different order, to help clarify your feelings;
- select from your writing any words or phrases that especially strike you, and use these as writing prompts to home in on exploring your feelings further;
- supplement your writing with a concluding prayer, to express a personal psalm-like progression towards God;
- switch to another writing mode to continue exploring and resolving what your writing is uncovering.

Writing around loss in other modes

Intuitive, sensing and reflective writing modes may support our writing through loss. Each can contribute to a shifting of perspective.

Where it is difficult, in a loss, to face feelings directly, an intuitive writing approach might help us start to express and explore it. Intuitive writing reaches into what is beyond our conscious awareness. Using it to write about loss may start with finding and writing around an image, as we alluded to in the last chapter. We may find our attention caught by something we see – a falling leaf, a stray dog, an empty chair. It might be an image in Scripture – a desert place, a lost coin. It might have a more obviously specific connection, such as a remembered moment or object that links us to a loved one in some way.

Mind-mapping, writing a paragraph, poem or even a fictional story around an image that resonates with our loss may help us release some deeper feelings without fear of being overwhelmed. We can approach them indirectly. Coming at our loss from this imaginative perspective may also release insights, aspects and angles that we had not seen before but that may help move us on.

A sensing writing mode, where we focus on factual detail, may help us in two ways. First, in writing about the facts of our current situation our perspective may become more balanced. In Chapter 3, Dorothy described making a list of what she had actually achieved on a difficult day, finding that these were things for which she could give thanks. Sometimes looking at our circumstances through a purely emotional lens can distort or dismiss the good that can be there.

Second, we may write about past events and what or who we have lost as a way of commemorating and celebrating what has been. We can preserve, through our writing, memories we want to keep and treasure.

A reflective writing mode primarily engages our head rather than our heart. We may want to use this sort of writing to process some of the implications of our loss. We may be asking difficult, searching and urgent questions:

- Why has this happened?
- Where is God in this?
- Who am I now?
- What do I believe now?
- How do I go forward from here?

Reflective writing is located in a more objective and wider per-spective than immediate, subjective experience. The very title of C. S. Lewis' book, *A Grief Observed*, where he explored his own grieving at his wife's death, encapsulates this approach. We may find ourselves writing in prose or even weighing up different sides of an argument in separate columns on the page.

Thinking through the meaning of our loss and integrating an understanding of it into our life and faith can take time. Reflective writing may come into its own *after* the raw feelings of a loss have begun to settle. As the immediate emotional storm – illness or health scare, redundancy, death or other sharp blow of disappointment – subsides, there may be more quiet space, without and within, to benefit from this writing mode.

Although these modes have been separated out above, they can interweave as we write our faith through our losses – expressing feelings, gaining insight, exploring meaning and grounding our-selves in how things are. We may also find some modes more helpful than others. There are no rules for how to use writing as part of healing through loss: different people use writing in different ways through different losses, as we shall see from the examples below.

Brian's story

Brian said he'd only occasionally used writing in his Christian life before his brother Ray died, aged 56. Ray was three years younger than Brian and apparently fit and healthy. He and Brian had enjoyed mountaineering together. Ray was diagnosed with cancer in December 2012. His condition worsened after a bad reaction to chemotherapy. He died on 2 February.

After the initial shock of the first few days, Brian felt a need to write. 'It came totally out of the blue and kept growing', he told me. 'It really took me by surprise.' As an outline formed in his mind, Brian hand-wrote several pages of notes and headings. Back home he typed these up on his computer and expanded them.

His resulting eight-page document, 'My Brother Ray: Some Memories, Thoughts and Reflections', comprises memories from childhood and their climbing expeditions; thoughts on Ray's character, in Brian's words and words copied from sympathy cards sent to the family; biographical dates and achievements; a spiritual reflection subtitled, 'Why do people climb?' Brian also included some Bible references, including Isaiah 40.31, a verse he said came to him when Ray died: 'I had a picture in my mind of him soaring up effortlessly, like the eagle, coming to rest in the heights of heaven.'

He did not record his feelings:

> I talked through my loss with others, so there was no need.
> I wrote to make sense of Ray's life and the special bond
> between us. It was always there, even though we didn't meet
> often, or chat much on our climbs.
>
> Because our mountain-climbing was just the two of us, I
> needed to objectify it in some way. I shared this writing with
> other family members, so I've a sense that my bond with Ray
> not only lives on in me, but with others who now know about
> it. I could acknowledge its significance for myself and before
> God, and I did. But I needed to include others too.
>
> The reflection helped me explore the spirituality of
> mountaineering. For me, climbing is an unconscious reaching
> out to God. Perhaps I was reassuring myself that Ray, who had
> a questioning faith, did have a personal relationship with God.

Brian said that completing this writing brought him some peace:

> Ray and I didn't really talk about what we'd done together and
> the bond we shared. We didn't need to say anything because
> we both understood it. But now he's gone, in a way my writing
> is my thank-you letter to Ray.

For Brian, recording facts and memories in black and white helped to recover a sense of permanence that seemed to have been taken away. His sensing and reflective writing brought some order and understanding to Ray's life, their brotherly bond and his engagement with his faith in the light of Ray's death. It is kept as both a thank you and a memorial to his brother.

Martin's writing responds to a loss of a different kind.

Martin's story

We encourage personal writing as part of the divorce recovery course I've been involved in running. Participants write their story for themselves in their own time. This remains private. We only ask that they be totally honest about what they did and how they feel. Generally, around half of them say that this writing was the most redemptive part of the course. It enabled them to look painful issues directly in the face.

Writing the story of my own marriage break-up helped me think more honestly about my part in it all. Writing allows you to put something out there. It's no longer gnawing away at you. Putting thoughts on paper brings them into focus. You can reflect, 'Is that how it was?' Forgiveness also comes into it. You can explore questions like, 'What am I forgiving the other for?' and 'Can I let go of this?'

Having a written record helps you move on. Healing can take time, but rereading what you've written several months later, you realize you don't feel like that any more.

Sometimes it helps to get rid of writing. As our course ends, we look at what people want to leave behind. They write these things down privately on pieces of paper. Then together, in silence, we put them on a bonfire outside.

Writing both about what had happened *and* how he felt helped Martin heal. By relocating the emotional pain on to paper he gained the objective distance he needed to ask himself some challenging questions about perception and forgiveness. Unlike Brian's memorial writing, the writing that Martin has kept is more of a marker, enabling him to see how far he has moved on from the loss rather than reconnecting him to it.

Living and writing through loss can be a more complex and ongoing process, as Dorothy's story illustrates.

Dorothy's story

Dorothy's husband was diagnosed with dementia seven years ago:

> It was the aggressive and violent kind. I looked after him
> at home until I had a mini heart attack. But he was totally
> unpredictable, with zero empathy, and I could get very low.
>
> When I tried saying prayers, I got lost in my head and was
> just burbling. I thought 'God deserves better than this'. I wanted
> to make sense, so I started writing my prayers. Life was impossible
> when my husband was diagnosed. I used to 'shout' at God in
> my journal using red ink and writing in capital letters all across
> the page. When I read it back much later, I was very embarrassed
> and felt very apologetic. But I sensed God saying that it was all right.

One morning, when Dorothy had settled her husband, she sat down for her quiet time but her Bible study notes brought no solace. 'They were clearly written by someone with a perfect life', she said. Unable to bear it any longer, Dorothy threw the booklet across the room with frustration.

> Then I felt God say something like, 'Well, you call yourself a
> writer. Why don't you write what you need today?' I thought,
> 'What *do* I need right now?' I just scribbled stuff down. The next
> day, I sensed a voice say 'Keep going. Do it for another day',
> so I did. It went on like this for a month. I realized that what
> I really wanted to know was that I wasn't on my own. Carers
> can suffer from depression as they're in a tunnel with no end.
> They need to see that they're not in a total vacuum.
>
> When I write, I feel I'm writing in God's presence, and also to
> him. He's the only other one there. Dialogue with God needs to
> be honest. The psalms opened it up for me. There are so many
> examples of the writer being very angry with God with no holds
> barred. God is the one person there's no point fudging things with.

Dorothy's writing is very much in the feeling mode: immediate, honest, emotional expression, even if it means 'shouting' in coloured capitals. It is primarily relational, and an integral part of her prayer-dialogue with God.

Dorothy does not remain stuck at the stage of venting emotions. Being directed to write her needs led to writing that demanded more objective observation and reflection – and that has eventually formed material to help other carers, in her book *One Day at a Time*.[3]

Mandy's writing charts her progress through a season of loss, step by step.

Mandy's story[4]

I've always kept a spiritual journal, not on a daily basis, but when key things happened in my life I tended to write about them or jot them down.

Three years ago I became ill with a progressive illness. It started with severe migraines but ended with me being confined to a wheelchair. My spiritual journal became my friend, as I wrote how I felt and what I thought God was teaching me day by day. The illness affected my memory, so I needed to write things down or else I'd forget. At my worst, I could hardly turn pages or hold books. I relied on God speaking to me through a daily perpetual calendar Scripture verse.

It was a struggle to write when I felt my body shutting down. I thought I was going to die, and even breathing became hard on some days. Yet at the same time I could be experiencing an inner peace and joy in God. One day I managed to write just three short sentences about this. It took me 20 minutes.

Breakthrough came when two friends fasted and prayed for my healing. Over the next four months, their prayers were answered.

As I reread my journals of that time – I'm writing a book on what I've gone through – I'm astonished at the things I wrote. It reminds me of how weak I was and how close and precious God was to me then. I wouldn't want that experience again, but writing has helped me reap its fruit and deepened my relationship with God.

If you're going through something, keep writing about what's happening as honestly as you can. You can have half an idea of what God might be saying to you, but as you write you start to understand it more fully. Writing about things as they're happening also helps you recognize when you've dealt with one level of an issue. You start finding a sense of peace as you write.

Like Dorothy's, Mandy's writing springs from a desire to stay connected to God through a season of loss and powerlessness. She was determined to keep writing, even when she could only manage three short sentences. Writing also kept her connected to herself, supporting her fragile memory.

Mandy's writing involves listening as well as expressing. She writes what she senses God is saying, to help her understand and discern it more clearly. She also listens to herself as she writes. Her writing is both a record and a resource for her Christian journey.

Mandy's healing restored what she had lost. Sally's loss brought different challenges.

Sally's story

Sally's life was turned upside down when her second son, Michael (now 23), was diagnosed with a severe/profound learning disability and autism.

> When children are born disabled, you've lost the child you dreamt of. There's no handbook for this. You want people to love the child that *is* there, so you try not to show your grief. There's loss, but life continues, and you just carry this grieving around inside you all the time.

Sally found herself wondering what was going on:

> The image I had of God did not work. I needed to readjust and come to terms with things. Children who are very challenging in terms of their behaviour throw up many questions about people and spirituality. How is the Spirit of God in that person? What did it mean to be given my son as a gift? I had so many 'why' questions about where God was in all this.

Sally struggled for resources with the substance to help her with the answers. Some supportive material for parents in her situation was written by non-Christians, while for her, some Christian material fell short on:

> the depth of the journey. I understood the crucifixion element of the faith, but with no cure for Michael, I saw no possibility of resurrection in my situation. In the end, I had to reach the point of despair. After that, I started seeing glimmers of resurrection and hope in all sorts of ways.

This process took Sally 13 years, and she said that writing helped her through:

> I wrote to feel my way through to being able to hold on to my faith and not let it slip away. When something rang true, I could write it down, so it was there to look back on later.

Sally had always written imaginative stories, a practice that helped sustain her through this period:

> Writing creatively was satisfying. It was using a gift I've been given, and the words stood there as a reminder that there was healing. On the whole, I wrote very short stories, just on a sheet of A4, about the next thing I'd discovered. You don't get a lot of time with a challenging child.

Sally wrote a children's story for her older son:

> He was experiencing the sorts of losses that children with disabled siblings face all the time – for instance, grieving that his younger brother would never play football with him. I wrote 'Coriolis' for him and 'Michael's Angel'[5] for his brother to explain God's involvement with him and with Michael, and his love for them both.

She also used story form to address this for herself:

> I wrote a story called 'Abandoned Love' about the day I was attacked by my son in the countryside, and realized I could no longer take him out by myself. It helped me process this in the light of my faith. Reflecting on my love for my son, even as he was hurting me, gave me a sliver of insight into God's passion for us in Jesus' suffering.[6]

> You have to have the courage to be honest, tell the story like it is, and invite God and others into your situation. Most of all you want to know you're not alone, but I chose carefully the people I told my stories to. Pain can be a doorway to God, but sometimes people don't know how to respond when hidden pain is disclosed.

Sally's loss threw her understanding of her faith 'out of the box'. Exploring aspects of her story imaginatively from different angles helped her to engage this tough, unfamiliar territory. A more intuitive approach in her writing led to the discovery of new spiritual connections. Gradually she reassembled her Christian faith with a depth of meaning that could sustain her.

Using even her limited opportunities to continue the writing that expressed her gifting and identity was affirming and supportive in itself.

Amid their different circumstances, some common features emerge among these Christians and their writing through loss.

- They felt alone with their loss, whether physically, emotionally, socially or spiritually. Talking to the page helped break that isolation.
- They felt disorientated by the upheaval in their circumstances and feelings. Putting something down in black and white validated their experience, making it an objective reality that could be engaged with.
- They wrote in various modes, using more than one approach: factual, reflective, emotional and imaginative. Both feelings and thoughts were included.
- They were honest. They used the page as a safe place to express exactly how things were, even if that took courage and meant a certain amount of discomfort.
- They interacted with their writing. They reread it and referred to it. They let it remind them, ask them questions and speak to them in new ways.
- They changed. Whether they found fresh insights, a recovered faith, a sense of peace, new hope or capacity to forgive, writing helped them move on in their journey with Christ.

Finally, in most cases they began to share their writing in some form with others, although we will think more about that in the last chapter.

Some things to try

Writing our surrender

In the stories above, an acceptance of situations that could not be controlled, fixed or even managed led to the beginnings of break-through, however tentative.

Whether our circumstances put us *in extremis* or we are in the ordinary course of life, Jesus' promise that 'those who lose their life for my sake will find it' (Matthew 10.39) still applies. We naturally like to be in charge of our own lives, but as the Christian writer John Ortberg observes, 'There is no way for a human being to come to God that does not involve surrender.'[7] This is not the retreat of a passive giving up but rather an active giving in to the one who made us, loves us and saves us.

Writing our surrender to God can help confirm our decision to give things over to him, and remind us, if we are wavering, that we have done so. We may also date our prayer to review later, to reflect on how God has acted in response. As John Ortberg comments, God always answers such a prayer, but in surrendering to him we give up any guarantee of a particular outcome.

If you wish to try a structured way of writing your surrender to God, complete the statement, 'I surrender . . .' or 'Lord, I give over to you . . .' Underneath write another sentence affirming an attribute of God, or copy out a Scripture verse that speaks of his faithfulness, as a reminder of the nature of the one to whom you are surrendering.

Verses you could choose could include:

- 'God is love' (1 John 4.16);
- 'The LORD, the LORD, a God merciful and gracious' (Exodus 34.6);
- 'Be still, and know that I am God!' (Psalm 46.10).

Or the words of Jesus, such as:

- 'Do not be afraid' (Mark 6.50);
- 'I am the good shepherd' (John 10.11);
- 'Follow me' (Luke 5.27);
- 'I will give you rest' (Matthew 11.28);
- 'Believe in God, believe also in me' (John 14.1).

Copying out God's word is a simple way of meditating on it as we attend more fully to each word. Old Testament Kings were instructed to write out God's laws personally, to impress his words on their hearts. In later centuries the copying out of God's word by monastic orders was a spiritual discipline that encouraged their contemplation of it. As you write out your verses, allow their meaning to become fully absorbed in your spiritual circulation.

Salvaged treasure: from 'If only' to 'And yet'

Sometimes we wish things were different. 'If only my family had not moved to New Zealand', said a lady at a writing workshop, 'Yet this has meant we've been out to visit a part of the world we'd otherwise never have seen.'

Accepting what we cannot change can enable us to catch the glimmers of God's redemptive work and goodness to us in the present moment. We open windows to receive God, rather than shutting the door on his love and our blessing. It can be challenging to look back at our life's 'If onlys'. We cannot change the past but we can allow the Lord to change us in relation to it.

Write the words 'If only . . .' at the top of your page, completing the sentence with whatever comes to mind. Underneath write 'And yet . . .', completing this sentence with something good that has come out of this.

God's 'And yets' are not a compensation for life's 'If onlys' but they can be a consolation. Salvaging these treasures through writing them down can remind us of their presence and God's grace.

10

Writing for growth

———◆◆◆———

Jan Dean went sleepwalking one night, dreaming about opening all her wardrobes and cupboards to discover:

> Birds. Bright birds.
> Day-Glo orange, flame yellow, jungle green,
> The turquoise of the seas of dreams.
> And when I open up the cupboard doors
> Out they fly – then follow
> As I wind my way
> Up through the house . . .

In Jan's dream, the emerging birds flutter through her home in 'a dazzle of feathers'. She walks upstairs as far as she can and opens the loft window:

> The cold night wakes me,
> Sharp with icy stars.
> While all around my dream birds fly
> And melt, escaping to the high black sky.

A year after having this dream, Jan used its images as the basis of her poem, 'Sleepwalking with Birds', quoted above. Four years after that, she discovered that the poem held a deeper resonance. She realized there was a connection between her actions in the dream and what she saw as the essence of her ministry as a Church of England Reader: setting people free. 'When you start to write, you step off a cliff', says Jan. 'A poem or story has a life of its own, and you meet things you didn't know were there.'

In this chapter we will explore more ways of using writing to seek spiritual growth: bringing our unconscious life into the light;

supporting us through spiritual direction or counselling; keeping us on track day-by-day; helping us move forward with vision and direction.

Writing with dreams

As Jan discovered, our sleeping life can be as active as our time awake. When we turn in for the night and our daytime defences go down, our deeper, unconscious life is free to express itself through our dreams.

God can interact with his Creation 24/7. The Bible contains many examples of him intervening in his people's sleep by speaking to them in dreams, all the way from Jacob to Joseph, the father of Jesus.

But even when God is not speaking directly, our own dream material can reveal insights we may have registered but pushed aside during the day; underlying concerns and issues to address; nudgings and desires that call for our attention.

Russ Parker, a Christian writer and extensive researcher on dreams, observes that 'the dream is a personal parable we have written to ourselves in order to send a basic message which we have been blind to in waking life'.[1]

Like a parable, a dream communicates in the language of images and symbols. These need some careful attention if we are to discern its meaning and message. Although Jan's vivid dream-image of the escaping birds stayed with her, the memory of a dream more often fades quickly on waking. If we want to be open to listening to our dreams, it can help to:

- write the dream down as soon as possible after waking. Some people keep a notebook and a small torch by their bedside to help them with this;
- write in the present tense, as if the dream is happening now, in as much detail as you can recall.

We have already considered the power of images and symbols as we looked at poetic writing. Understanding our dream's message involves exploring the images and symbols our unconscious has created and their uniquely personal meaning for us. People, things and places familiar in our waking life may assume a particular significance in our dream's landscape and drama.

Further writing can help us explore the dream. Here are some things to try.

- Describe your feelings in the dream. Do these resonate with any similar feelings in your waking life? What are these connections and what might they be telling you? Is the dream signposting something in your daily life that you need to address? Jot down your thoughts for prayer and reflection.
- Write down any key images – such as the colourful birds, cupboards and loft window in Jan's dream – and mind-map any associations they have for you.
- Write a dialogue between you and an object or person in the dream that particularly intrigues or puzzles you. Often these elements represent some aspect of ourselves. What questions do you want to ask them? What will they say in response? Seek to listen to them, and write what comes to mind. An insight may surface as you write or read over your material.
- Write down any links that occur to you between the dream events, images or symbols and any Bible verses, stories or wise Christian words spoken to you that spring to mind.

Dreams, particularly those that break off abruptly, can indicate unfinished business.

If you find this unsettling, it may be helpful to talk and pray with a Christian friend to support you in resolving what has emerged.

Daytime doorways

While our dreams may be, as Freud observed, 'a royal road to our unconscious at night', the stuff of our daily lives may provide pointers to areas for personal growth. A river's flow is not glassily smooth. Ripples and bubbles, swirls and currents disturb the surface, indicating the presence of unseen rocks or fish beneath.

The things that ruffle our calm as we go through the day can alert us to the presence of something lurking underneath. It may be a long-unresolved issue or an aspect of ourselves that makes us feel uncomfortable. For example, if we come from a home where conflict was always avoided, we may find it hard to face anger in ourselves. We may have learned to push it back down inside us, into the shadows, and even deny it altogether. Sometimes we may deal with it by attributing it to another person, describing them as being angry when it is we who are enraged.

Christian wholeness involves bringing every part of us into the light, however 'unacceptable'. We may encourage this by praying the psalmist's prayer, 'Search me, O God, and know my heart' (Psalm 139.23), and asking for discernment to see signs of our shadow territory revealing itself. We can gain glimpses of what is under our surface in the flash of our reactions to the situations or behaviour that 'presses our buttons'.

Pressed buttons

Explore this by drawing some large circles on a piece of paper to represent your buttons – when they get pressed, it triggers your reaction. Inside each button write what or who it takes to press it. If you find this hard, the questions listed here might help.

- What is it about others that especially gets under my skin?
- Whom do I find really irritating, and what is it about them that I react to?
- Whom do I really admire/envy and what is it about them that I aspire to?
- Where do I find myself overreacting to a minor situation?
- What do I always seem to put off doing?
- What was taboo to talk about in our family circle?
- What could my parents do that would most annoy me?

The last two questions around family life can reveal significant material connected to our upbringing. It has been said that our parents know best how to push our buttons because they installed them.

Choose a button to write about and explore in more depth, seeking to discover what makes its pressing so painful. Write honestly into this area until you sense you have identified something of the root cause beneath the current issue. See your writing as a prayer that brings this area into God's light. Make space to listen and write what you sense God may be calling you to do as a next stage towards wholeness. You may wish to ask a trusted friend for prayer support in this.

Sarah, a young mother and teaching assistant, said she found it 'thought-provoking' to address these questions in relation to family life. 'You think things through in more detail when you're writing them down', she said. She even added in a question of her own: 'Is there a person or situation where you're most likely to reveal your weakness?'

Sarah found herself writing reflectively about an incident with her three-year-old son:

> I took away Josh's toys for bad behaviour, when in fact his behaviour wasn't 'bad'. We were both tired. I didn't have much patience and I treated him unfairly. This linked back to issues around my own upbringing. Without criticizing the parenting I received, I like to think I'm a bit more flexible and understanding. I'm disappointed when I'm not. Working with children with special needs, I often see the implications of unfair and, in some cases, poor parenting. It's always on my mind and I pray for guidance about it on a regular basis.

Writing for growth in spiritual direction

At various times in this book I have suggested the value of talking or praying through issues that your writing may have brought to the fore. But writing our faith can also be done in conjunction with support already in place, such as spiritual direction or counselling. Writing may be useful as basic preparation for a session, as it is for Sue:

> I have spiritual direction four times a year. Before it, I go through my appointments diary over the previous few months and jot down in lists the key things I've been doing. If I've been very busy, I tend to forget some of them. Writing gathers everything together in a form that I can see. It's a two-hour

drive to see my spiritual director, so I can use that as thinking time. The writing beforehand provides a focus.

Ricarda's preparatory writing is not just for herself:

I write to my spiritual director before we meet. I put on paper what's going on within me, and what I think God's doing in my life – not lists of activities. This covers a lot of groundwork beforehand, and I approach our meeting in a less 'helter-skelter' frame of mind. My life is better, and I become more truly available to others when I take the time to reflect on what's going on.

Writing helps me see things. By taking the words out of my head and getting them on paper, I can see. In my head I don't see so much.

For Andrew, the writing is not just preparatory but gains an exploratory dimension within the session itself:

My spiritual direction sessions have increasingly become a time where we take a poem I've written and read it together. It's like a spiritual literary exercise really, opening up the text of my life. I find out uncomfortable things that my poem says to my own heart.

Writing, for me, is a way of exploring and constructing my relationship with God. As I attend to the stuff of my life, I find words and meaning in it. Then I find the spiritual within that, which takes me into even deeper purpose and meaning.

Writing can also be a fruitful activity after a session of spiritual or therapeutic support. As a Christian undergoing cognitive behavioural therapy in a secular context, Lesley found writing helpful both personally and as a means of engaging spiritual support:

I had two Christian friends who supported me. They'd know when I was having an appointment. I wrote after each counselling session, reflecting on what we talked about, my tasks and objectives for the week, and how I could tackle them prayerfully. Then I'd write these out in summary form as an email to my friends, along with my specific prayer requests.

My therapist respected me and worked with my ideology, but being committed to producing something in writing for my two praying friends meant that I created and maintained a spiritual framework for the whole process. This was an equally important part of the therapy.

Keeping on track

Lesley told me that writing to inform her friends' prayers sprang from a desire for accountability. If we have a similar desire, we may find that journalling a daily examen could be a helpful structure for personal writing that helps us stay on our spiritual tracks.

The daily examen is a characteristic feature of Ignatian spirituality (examen being the Spanish word for 'examine'). Over 400 years ago, St Ignatius of Loyola encouraged this reflective prayer exercise to review the day's events and discern God's presence and direction. His original five prayer-steps could be reworked as prompts for your own writing.

1 **Become aware of God's presence.** Write about where/when you most sensed God's presence today.
2 **Review the day with gratitude.** List some blessings you want to give thanks for today.
3 **Pay attention to your emotions.** Write about a significant emotion you have had during the day. What might God be saying through this feeling?
4 **Choose one feature of the day and pray from it.** Ask the Holy Spirit to direct you to what God thinks is important in this day. Write to explore what might be making this significant in God's eyes.
5 **Look towards tomorrow.** Choose one aspect or challenge that faces you tomorrow and write your prayer about it.

Another five-a-day . . .

Just as our bodies need fruit and vegetables to stay well, thankfulness is an essential part of a good spiritual diet. Paul's encouragement to the Ephesian Christians to be 'giving thanks to God the Father at all times and for everything' (Ephesians 5.20) is a message he underlines in letters to other Christian fellowships.

Just the simple, regular practice of listing your five-a-day can set the day in perspective and deepen your awareness of God's provision. You may wish to try this for a season. In our home, we've found that telling each other about our five-a-day over the evening meal also leads to some good conversations – sometimes we have to remind each other that it's *only* five!

Looking around

One way of catching hold of your five-a-day as they come is to adopt the writers' practice of carrying a notebook around with you. Having a notebook handy enables you to write:

- a prayer as you drink a cup of coffee;
- an inner hunch or nudge that you sense might be from God;
- a need or issue you notice to pray for;
- a focused description of something in a quiet moment to sharpen your senses;
- a Bible verse that keeps coming to mind;
- a theme that keeps recurring in your day;
- an overheard comment or a quote you read that catches your attention;
- ideas, phrases, reflections you might wish to follow up in writing later.

Sally says that if she has a thought she wants to keep when she is out and about, without pen and paper to hand:

> I speak it into my phone, using the recording function. I don't lose so much that way. I keep it short and then listen back to a whole batch every so often. Then I write down the bits that still catch my attention.

As the Christian writer Richard Rohr has said, 'God comes to us disguised as our lives.' We can easily miss God's presence through inattention or busyness. Reflective writing can help us slow down to attune ourselves to where God is at work. You may want to take some quiet moments to write your response to a question such as 'Where have I been tripping over God lately?' in whatever form appeals – paragraphs, list, mind-map or poem. Afterwards, read over what you have written and use further writing to answer the questions listed here.

- How many different ways does God's presence come alongside me?
- Are some ways more prominent than others?
- Which am I most likely to miss at the time?
- Which do I seem to be most aware of at the time?
- How could I live so I'm more aware of God's presence throughout the day?
- What response am I being called to make through these experiences?

Reviewing our journey

As we write our faith journey, we start to build up something of a Christian travel diary. Reviewing this writing from time to time can be fruitful. You may wish to do this monthly or quarterly, at particular seasons – Advent or Christmas, Lent or Easter – or make it part of time set aside on retreat.

Lesley rereads her journal monthly and reviews it methodically. She writes a brief summary of its key content, listing under various headings such aspects as personal achievements, events, spiritual teaching and reflections on positive and negative experiences. She then bases her annual review on these 12 summaries.

My own reviews are not so impressively organized! I read back to see what strikes me, jotting down what feels important in one list. For me, it feels especially important to note and reflect on anything I still need to attend to, or that suggests the direction and priorities I need to set for the way ahead.

Reading over a faith journal can trigger many responses: I can feel relieved or thankful at the outcome of something; amazed at how agitated I felt about what is no longer an issue; excited to be reminded of some wisdom I'd noted but forgotten; dismayed at where I seem to be stuck in a rut. Any or all of these may prompt written reflections and prayers, as the page becomes a milestone on my Christian journey.

Some questions to prompt writing as you review your Christian journey

- Who is God to me today and how has he been with me over these last months?
- How have I and/or my circumstances changed, and what does this mean for me?
- Where have I and/or my circumstances remained the same, and does this signify stability or stagnation?
- Where am I being called to make endings or beginnings?
- Where am I being called to continue and persist?
- Where am I looking for life as I journey on?
- How would I describe the heart of my God-given vocation?
- What do I hear as God's word(s) for me at this moment?

Growing in knowledge

Throughout this book we have looked at the value of engaging *both* feeling *and* thinking in writing our faith. While the emphasis has been more on a writing approach that starts with feelings and moves towards thinking, those among us most at home with loving God with all their minds may find a more natural progression the other way around. For Jane and Jerry, seeking knowledge and exploring understanding in writing opened up new levels of connection:

I use writing as part of my spiritual discipline. I don't necessarily address things to God, but I write about God. I find God extremely exciting.

I tend not to know what I think until I've written it down, so I write theology as a way of clarifying my own thinking. This sort of writing is sporadic. I may scribble in a notebook and not look at it again. Sometimes I keep what I've written. I start writing, just as things occur to me, for their own sake, although if enough things connect up, it may form the basis of some lecture notes.

Recently, at a Sunday Eucharist, a passage written on the Eucharist by the Victorian liturgist Dom Gregory Dix came to mind. I looked it up and wrote some of it out. I carried on writing about different Eucharistic situations throughout history, Jesus' parables on the banquet and his own institution of the Eucharist. Words are very much part of the vision of what the Eucharist is.

As I wrote the words out and put these different strands of thinking together on the page, the connections helped me explore the theological significance and shape of the liturgy. The act of physically writing such words is incarnational, and I participate differently in the Eucharist as a result. *Jane*

I went to Israel, thinking that in Jesus' land I'd feel close to him, but as I looked down over Capernaum from above the Sea of Galilee, I realized that if Jesus were to walk along there at that moment I'd have no point of contact with him. I'd not be able to speak his language and his culture would be completely different.

Back home I wondered what it would have been like for some of the Gospel characters who saw Jesus – the hidden people at the edge of events, like Zacchaeus or Peter's mother-in-law. I imagined looking through their eyes, and tried to distil the voice of the person seeing Jesus into a few sentences of reflection on the impact he made.

Through writing about an encounter with Christ as a human being in a specific time and place, I discovered that what mattered most was not his ethnicity but his shared humanity. This was transformative. I no longer felt distant from Jesus but much more connected.

The writing was important. If I write something and I get the phrase right, I come back to it later and it says something to me that I didn't know I knew. It brings a new understanding only expressible in those particular words. In the end, I met Jesus in a different space and place from where I'd expected. *Jerry*

The thoughts and questions stimulating Jane's and Jerry's writing took them back to scriptural and theological texts. There is much published material available to support our studying of God's word. By writing as well as reading, this study can be more effective. We reinforce what we are learning and open ourselves to engaging with it more thoughtfully. If you are reading the Bible, you may wish to jot down:

- particular words, phrases or verses that speak to you;
- thoughts that surface as you read;
- questions you would want to ask of God and the passage;
- connections that occur to you – with other writings, your own life and circumstances;
- how you would want your life to be different through reading this passage.

Any or all of these may be followed up in further writing.

God also speaks through his world as well as his word. You may find yourself reading, watching or hearing something in which a phrase or an incident seems to carry a resonance for you: a line in a book or an image in a film; a conversation or comment; an incident or something you see around you. Writing things down as you reflect on them may help you track your thinking as you explore the insight.

Writing forward

The Scriptures are full of encouragement to look forward in our faith journey. In the New Testament, Paul pictures himself as a runner, fixing his eyes on the finishing line as he presses on 'towards the goal for the prize of the heavenly call of God in Christ Jesus' (Philippians 3.14). Having a forward-looking dimension to writing our faith may help 'envision' us – energize and inspire us with hope – as we face challenges and seek to discern our direction ahead.

Opening our eyes

If we are feeling daunted by a situation that we have to face, we tend to see it through the magnifying glass of our anxieties. Some writing may help us identify and take courage from the resources God has put in place for us to meet it.

When King Aram's mighty army surrounded the city of Dothan in pursuit of Elisha, the prophet was not dismayed. He prayed for his servant to see God's protecting heavenly host ranged behind these hostile forces. His prayers were answered, and Elisha was not captured (2 Kings 6.9–23).

Write a paragraph about a situation you face but feel inadequate to meet as a Christian. It could be a particular challenge or an ongoing situation, such as with a family member or in your workplace. Write both specifically about your event or issue *and* your feelings about it.

Now ask the Lord to open your spiritual eyes to the resources in place for you, within or beyond the obvious physical circumstances. As things come to mind, write your response to the questions:

- What has God provided – spiritually, materially, socially or in any other way – to equip me in this situation?
- How does seeing these things affect my response, my prayers and my actions?

You may find, as I did, that more resources occur to you as you continue writing. The advantage of writing these down is that you can:

- reread it to remind yourself of God's resources if you need encouragement;
- record any further resources you realize later that God has also provided;
- review any commitments you made in the light of it, to hold yourself accountable.

Writing our guidance

The most helpful image I've ever heard to describe God's guidance is that of landing lights. When a pilot lands an aircraft at night, lights along the runway beneath are vital. A single light is not sufficient to risk an approach – a succession is needed, providing an illuminated pathway to enable the pilot to align the aircraft and land safely.

If we sense God calling us to set foot on new territory of some kind, we may find ourselves looking for spiritual 'landing lights' to confirm his leading, especially if this change has significant implications. God's landing lights may line up as a combination of various elements: circumstances; words of Scripture, others' insights, 'chance' remarks, something we read or see that catches our attention; an inner hunch, conscience or desire.

Landing lights

If you are sensing a holy nudge to move forward in some direction – change of occupation, new ministry or venture from joining a mission team to taking on a foster child – writing down the landing lights of guidance as they emerge can help build your faith and confidence of solid ground ahead.

Take a blank page to designate it as a 'runway'. Write at the top or in the middle what you sense you are being guided into, and then list or mind-map any landing lights already in the picture. You may want to line them up on the page.

You can add to this page over time as, if and when more 'lights' appear. It can also be useful to look back over it, open to any other confirming indicators that you may have missed. As you do so, be open to whether you now have sufficient lighting for a spiritual landing or whether a different pattern is emerging. Keep weighing your insights against scriptural principles, to explore if, like Gideon (Judges 6.33–39), you are ready to be obedient but seek assurance, or are looking for surplus lights as a way of avoiding action.

Garnering future wisdom

The conference speaker had inadvertently pressed my 'angry button'. I felt I was justified: she had disappointed her audience by failing to address the talk's publicized topic. But beneath this good reason lurked the real reason for my reaction. Something she said was yet another landing light to let go of a particular line of work and make more space for creative and therapeutic writing. I was resisting hard. As Gillie Bolton notes, 'change cannot come without a degree of discomfort accompanied by a sense of vulnerability',[2] and I was not yet up for this.

What I already knew but didn't do ended up costing me unnecessary stress. A year later I reached a point of overload. Something had to go, and I finally ended that work commitment with a huge sense of relief.

We often live our lives in limbo between what we know we need to put into action and what we are actually doing. As Mark Twain famously quipped, 'It ain't those parts of the Bible that I can't understand that bother me, it is the parts that I do understand.' Sometimes we do not want to face the things we know, so we push them to the edge of our consciousness, hoping that out of sight will be out of mind.

One way to unearth some of these things can be to write a letter from your future self to yourself now. Writing can move us backwards and forwards like a time machine. Writing as our future self may help us to be more receptive to the wisdom and guidance that the Holy Spirit has already planted within us. The writer Nancy Kline, who encourages effective listening and thinking in organizations, suggests seeking to identify 'what we already know now that we are going to find out in a year's time'.[3]

Imagine yourself a year ahead, or whatever time-jump is appropriate: if you have a planned transition coming up, such as getting married, moving, having a baby, retiring, it may affect when you want to position your letter-writing. Give your letter a future date and consider including:

- what you want your present self to know;
- what difference this knowledge may be making to your future self;
- what advice or encouragements you want to give your present self;
- what you want to tell your present self you are doing or have done.

You may wish to keep the letter to review when the date of writing arrives in reality. How might what you have written affect what you do tomorrow? Or even today?

For reflection

1 Reflect on your writing rhythm.

  - Do you want to keep your personal writing in a particular place and review it at regular points in the month or year?
  - How do you want to integrate personal writing into your Christian life?

2 Review any writing exercises you have tried in this book.

  - Which worked best for you and which were more of a challenge?
  - Which have been the most illuminating or fruitful?
  - Which would you like to explore further?
  - Do you prefer to write in a structured or spontaneous way?
  - Do you start more naturally with expressive feeling or reflective thinking as you write?

11

Writing to, with and for others

—◆◇◆—

'When my friend was going through a tough time, I wanted to make her birthday special', Stef told me. She decided to compose a poem to encourage her friend, and write it out on a scroll of paper, tied up with ribbon, for her friend to keep. 'I felt that was more special than just a card with "God Loves You" printed on it', she said.

Stef had written poetry before but 'this was the first time I'd ever sat down intentionally to ask God to help me write something encouraging for someone else'. Her prayers were answered:

> Pictures started coming to mind. Six years earlier, I'd been in a church mission team, going to Romania. Someone said God had a word for me, that I was a rosebud in God's garden, and he was tending me. This had little resonance for me at the time, but I remembered it as I was writing the poem. I saw my friend as God's watering can. I replaced the flowers with weeds, to fit the rhyme.
>
> The story of Ruth also came to mind – how she looked to Boaz for protection as he spread out his cloak. My image was of Jesus putting his protective cloak over my friend. This sort of language and picture was a bit fanciful for me, but I was creating this poem as a gift, to express love and friendship.

Our Christian journey is not purely a solo venture. Our faith is rooted in relationship – with God, others and our environment, as well as ourselves. Although our private writing may be part of a change in us that affects others, we may also wish to use our writing more directly with others. In this chapter we will look at some ways of writing our faith with or for others: to encourage and bless; deepen our relationships; write together for fun; reach out more widely.

Writing to encourage and bless

Stef created her poem to make something in words to encourage and bless her friend. Even if we do not feel able to write a poem, we can use personal words in other forms to do the same job. We have already looked at the power of letters as encouragers of others. The next time you catch yourself thinking how well someone has done, appreciating some aspect of them or sensing a Bible verse coming to mind in your prayers for them, write it down and pass it on. You may like to keep a small stock of attractive cards and notelets for the purpose.

Written encouragements can become treasured keepsakes, perhaps coming even more into their own at a later time when affirming words are especially needed. They can also help underline the positive for those of us too inclined to brush off or play down spoken compliments.

Writing our appreciation to our nearest and dearest, who often see us when we are most frayed at the edges, can also be very precious. Expressing positive input can help draw us closer together in our everyday lives. Paul urges the Philippian Christians to focus on whatever is lovely and good (Philippians 4.8–9) but it can take a crisis to release those words of love. Why risk the wait, when none of us really knows how long we have to communicate what really matters?

Some marriage refreshment courses, including the one we went to a few years ago, include a letter-writing exercise. On our weekend we were to write letters of appreciation on the Sunday morning. Husbands then brought a tray of coffee to their wives in their room, and each read out their letter to the other. Once I overcame the oddness of writing to someone I actually lived with, it was a highly affirming exercise.

Love letters to spouses need not be confined to courses. They can be written at other meaningful times, such as anniversaries or on Valentine's Day, on fine handmade paper; shorter, loving messages can be written on sticky notes attached to mirrors or computer screens, or on cards tucked into lunch-boxes or under pillows to be discovered later. The main thing is that your writing is personal, positive, authentic and specific.

We can also write to our children. Words that come our way when we are young have great potential to shape us for good or ill, so it is important to bless the upcoming generation.

To bless is to commend someone to God's favour as a prayer for their well-being, happiness and prosperity in every sense. The organization Focus on the Family encourages parents to write personal blessings for their children, to include:

- affirming their worth;
- envisaging a positive and God-filled future for them;
- expressing love and care to support the blessing's fruition.[1]

I hesitated to suggest this to Robin and Vicky, parents in their early thirties with three daughters: two-year-old Florence, six-year-old Madeleine and eight-year-old Olivia. With two jobs – Vicky as a teacher, Robin as a vet – and an active church life, I wondered when this busy couple would find the time to write. Both responded enthusiastically, however, deciding each to write a blessing for one of their older daughters.

When it came actually to writing a blessing to share with her child face-to-face, Vicky was surprised to feel 'terrified. I wondered how Livy would react. Would she be embarrassed? Would she show it to her friends? Would she reread it in ten years' time and cringe?'

Vicky and Robin typed their blessings and printed them out. 'Ideas were slow to start with', said Robin. 'I wondered how to get the spiritual side in. I wrote that Maddy was a gift from God. The words came more easily as I went on. I focused on Maddy's personality traits and qualities.'

Vicky avoided being too specific about her hopes for Livy's future:

I wouldn't want her to think she'd disappointed me if she did not marry and have children. I knew these were words I couldn't take back. I was explicit in how proud I am of Livy, her sensitive and caring nature, and how much I love her.

Reading this to Livy was not as awkward as Vicky had feared. For Robin, 'It felt natural to share my blessing with Maddy. She seemed very moved and even cried what she called "happy tears".'

Maddy confirmed how good she had felt: 'It was really nice. I know I'm loved but there were more things in the blessing.' Livy said that hearing hers gave her a 'wobbly feeling in my tummy. It was lovely. I read it again sometimes.' Both girls have asked for their blessings to be framed.

While Vicky regularly tells her children daily that she loves them, in spur of the moment affection, writing felt different: 'It helped me focus on the important things in their lives. It also made me reflect on my promises to them as a mother.'

Robin said:

Sometimes you feel you spend all your time with the children just engaged in the daily activities like homework, getting dressed, baths, meals or telling them off. Taking time to focus on their positive attributes and remind myself that they were given to us by God was really refreshing and energizing.

Writing with others

As well as writing for others on our Christian journey, we may write with others:

- to experience or explore ways of writing for Christian growth;
- to share and develop our God-given creativity by writing together.

When I told our small fellowship group that we were going to write cinquains for our reflective worship, there were some scarcely concealed groans of dismay. Karen thought she would have to think up rhymes. Penny and Sue winced at memories of miserable times slogging at poetry in a school classroom. Simon, who is dyslexic, said he felt pressured. I took a deep breath, handed out sheets explaining what cinquains were, and said the idea was to help us settle, focus and discover how creative we could be. To my relief, the group graciously agreed to give it a go.

I had set out some objects on a tray for everyone to choose from: a wooden cross, glass angel, cup, flower, key and a reel of cotton.

Alan said he wanted to write about something else. The room soon felt surprisingly quiet as people became absorbed in the task of looking, listening and writing.

Afterwards, I invited anyone who wished to to read out their poems. Once Karen had taken the plunge as the first reader, others followed. 'Hearing other people's cinquains made me realize that mine was OK', said Penny. By now Alan had written three.

Sue was stuck for a last word on hers. The group offered some suggestions. Penny noticed her object's contrasting features: 'I was struck by how cotton is strong, but then I saw fragility as well. Writing the poem made me realize how often I look at things and don't really see them. I had to stop and think, "What does it actually do?"'

The group moved on to that evening's topic – Christians as a mouthpiece for truth and justice. We seemed to have left the activity behind, but as we discussed how our anxieties about speaking out were often groundless when we rose to the challenge, Penny said, 'That's just what I felt when you said we were going to write a poem. I thought it would be really hard, but when it came down to it I could actually do it.'

Our group's cinquains included two angels. Alan focused on coffee.

Coffee
Black and bitter
Inviting, stimulating, refreshing
The midnight encounter anticipated and enjoyed
Nectar!

Angel
Winged, solemn
Challenging, frightening, comforting
The unseen overseer of all we are and do
Servant

Angel
Clear and light
Standing, blessing, beautifying
Your elegant presence brings me joy
Messenger

Meeting to write

If we are meeting as a writing group rather than fellowship group, it helps to be clear about aims, particularly about whether the focus is more on encouraging the writers or working on the writing itself. This is very important if participants' writing discloses feelings about personal issues that are live and current for them.

More than Writers has been meeting for well over two years. We meet about once a month, not always on the same day each time. It started with Mandy, who founded it, putting a message out around our church asking if there were any amateur writers interested in joining a group.

There are about eight to ten of us, with about five to six usually around at any one meeting. We discuss the projects we have going currently. Some of us are writing books. Others write just for fun. We talk about what we're writing, the difficulties and the issues. We'd all like to have books published!

Sometimes we set ourselves homework, such as a writing exercise to bring along to the next meeting. It could be writing a story that has to include a particular sentence, say, or uses the colour green as a prompt.

We try to be constructive in our feedback. We listen to one another's writing in an accepting environment. I used to write casually for my own recreation. The first time I'd ever shared my writing was in the group. Positive feedback enables you to be more confident. It gave me the courage to start up my blog.

We also pray together at the end of our meeting and discuss our faith quite a lot.

My advice for starting a Christian group is to make it a warm and welcoming place. Be friends first. Try to create a relaxed atmosphere, but make sure the meetings have a structure.

Andrew[2]

A Christian writer once told me how people would show him poems about profound spiritual experiences, yet as they talked to him they described their experiences in language far more vivid than that of their poems. In ironing out their writing, they had flattened its expression and lost something of its heart.

One way of supporting each other in drawing out our most creative writing could be to pair up with a friend who will scribe your exact words on your subject as you speak them out – and vice versa. This can help catch your best words while they are still alive, before Inner Critics or Censors have had time to get to work.

Some guidelines for a Christian faith-writing group

- Clarify where your aims lie in terms of effective writing and personal growth.
- Establish trust and confidentiality.
- Be prayerful and enjoy fellowship, but don't become distracted from writing.
- Be sensitive to the vulnerability members may feel about sharing writing.
- Encourage members to talk about the writing process, not just the product.
- Ask what the writing means to the writer.

Writing more widely

Although there is an overlap between private and public writing, there are some important differences. Personal writing for ourselves or God alone, to explore, learn, worship or foster healing, works best where we can put words on the page as free of judgement or constraints of correctness as possible.

Sharing our writing with others – even those we know – means considering not only what we want to express but how it will be read and received. This may mean working on our writing, honing what it is we want to communicate into the most effective way of writing it.

Writing for a wider group, including those we have perhaps never met, may involve greater effort. We can make fewer assumptions about readers we do not know. Our writing may need redrafting, shaping, clarifying with grammatical and syntactical accuracy. We may need a more critical eye to look at our writing objectively.

Allowing others to see our writing exposes our naked words on the page. We may want to choose carefully when and with whom we share our most personal writing. As readers we may need to tread gently if invited to read another's personal writing, and focus on understanding what it means to the writer, as well as affirming what we genuinely find effective or striking.

Blogging

The advice goes, 'Put all your heart into a piece of personal writing. Take it out again if you want to work on it for publication.' But what does it mean to publish our writing?

The growth of internet and social media, alongside the rise of self-publishing, makes it increasingly easy to disseminate our writing worldwide as soon as we have created it. A blog website ('blog' being a portmanteau word comprised of 'web' and 'log') enables the blogger to 'post' their expertise or experience, interests or insights, whenever they wish, and invites readers to respond with comments and feedback. In 2006 a survey by the US company NM Incite tracked 36 million bloggers worldwide. By the end of 2011 this had risen to over 181 million blogs. Their research also indicated that more women blog than men and that half of all bloggers are aged between 18 and 34. Some 50 per cent are parents and the majority are college or university educated.

Whether we write specifically Christian blogs or more generally blog as Christians, we need to be aware of the nature of this writing genre. In its interactive set-up, blogging has the feel of writing for others. Personal blog-posts also tend to be informal in style, reading more like diary entries or one-sided conversations than articles. All this creates a sense of personal relationship – but it is not quite that simple.

Blog-writing is likely to be a private activity; whatever is published, however, is accessible immediately to anyone with a computer, and unlike a one-off conversation, a blog-post becomes a permanent on-screen record.

The interactive nature of blogging links people across great distances but it may not necessarily connect them. When writing alone on to a screen, our attention may be so caught up in what we are expressing – especially if we feel passionately about an issue – that we lose sight of the fact that we are potentially talking to the whole world.

Digital disconnection operates both ways. If we risk losing an awareness of those reading our online communication, we may also be at the receiving end of others' words that show little consideration for our human vulnerabilities.

Blogging in particular and writing in social media in general also raise questions around our identity and integrity, as Christians called to walk in the light. For example:

- Do we expose our authentic selves online or post behind a persona?
- Are we prepared to say what we are posting, face-to-face, with anyone?
- Are we limiting what we say out of discretion or deception?
- In writing about or to others, are we exercising compassion and courtesy?
- How does our writing line up with Paul's injunction to the Philippians (4.8)?

The time-lag between writing and publishing is far shorter online than with a hard-copy publication. This may be a pitfall because generally speaking the more people you hope will read your writing, the more attention you will need to have given it first. So take your time. A first draft where you put your passions on to the page may later look quite different to you. You may be glad you did not expose it to a wider viewing at its earliest stage.

As a Christian blogger, think about the language you use. Seeking to communicate to a circle beyond those who are like-minded may affect the words you choose. Little and often is also a key phrase for this genre. You may need to redraft and shorten articles to make them more effective.

> I was guest-blogging on alcohol issues on others' sites, and my faith was creeping through. It was a key part of my recovery from alcoholism, but I didn't want to come over as 'God Squad'. However, readers started responding and asking me to write more. This gave me confidence to start my own blog, and use my personal side in writing in a new way.
>
> My blog started off as motivational and about well-being. It's important to be your authentic self and find your own voice. Write for you, but be aware of your audience. If you're writing publicly, don't write what you might later regret, or anything that you wouldn't discuss with anyone face to face. Your growing children might read what you've written one day.
>
> I don't find it difficult to write personally on my blog. I was in a Christian re-hab centre 14 years ago, and no stone was left unturned in my life. I've nothing left to hide or work through. Knowing you're forgiven is a powerful position to be in.
>
> *Carolyn*[3]

Writing in perspective

As we draw towards the end of looking at personally writing our faith, it is worth making two points. First, writing takes an effort; second, although it can be of great value for us, it is not the only tool for Christian spiritual growth.

Choosing to write, like many decisions we make in our Christian lives, demands being intentional. Most things worth doing in life call for something from us. As the writer to the Hebrews says, 'discipline always seems painful rather than pleasant at the time, but later it yields the peaceful fruit of righteousness', when we are trained by it (Hebrews 12.11).

The disciplines of our Christian life, such as worship, praying and Bible reading, also call for an intentional approach. Writing may be part of that but it is not compulsory!

If some of the writing exercises or the process of writing in general do not work for where and who you are on your Christian journey, do not worry.

Also, although we have been looking at writing that involves others, it is emphatically not the case that the only marker of value for our writing is the range of its readership. Writing that is entirely personal and private can accomplish a powerful purpose on our faith journey. Ultimately all human words ever written will pass away. Only what God writes on our hearts and into us through our reading and writing is for keeps. Writing, like any other activity, needs to be in balance with the rest of our Christian lives.

Too little writing and we lose the opportunities it offers for creativity, reflection and focus on our Christian journey. There is much to gain from slowing down to become fully attentive, explore issues, grow our creativity, offload feelings, think things through, express our worship, strengthen our learning and renew our vision. It can sometimes be a joy to write – at other times a discipline – as we go in search of a deeper spiritual life and its riches.

Too much writing and we may end up as mere spectators of life, standing back from full involvement and commitment. Even committed writers do not produce their best if they try to fill every available hour with writing. Times away from the page and engaged in wider living contribute as much to our creative process as sitting down to write. We sometimes need to let go, leave our writing to return to it later with fresh perspective and discernment. Writing is more like gardening than working on a production line: it needs a rhythm of both attention and rest in order to grow.

At the end of John's Gospel the writer tells us intriguingly that there were many other things that Jesus said and did that could not be contained in all the books in the world if they were to be written down (John 21.25). The early Christians did not try to record all of Jesus' words and actions. Writing their faith meant, for them, writing enough to point us to the living Word and then living in relationship with him. As we come to the end of these words, we might note, in the spirit of the writer of Ecclesiastes, that there is:

a time to write and a time to cease from writing;
a time to keep our writing and a time to destroy it;
a time to hide our writing and a time to share it;
a time to work on our writing and a time to see it as
 completed;
a time to reread it and a time to leave it be.

The New Testament uses the image of the written decree to re-assure those putting their trust in Jesus of their destiny. Our names are written in heaven (Luke 10.20) and recorded in the book of life to be opened on Judgement Day (Revelation 13.8). Christians themselves become divine writing material. Under the New Covenant, God's Laws are to be written on our hearts. However we write our faith, may we allow the living Word to write his story into our lives, and our lives into his bigger story, as we become an open invitation letter to those as yet outside the kingdom (2 Corinthians 3.3).

Some things to try

1 Consider pairing up with a friend to encourage each other in writing your faith. Share ideas and experiences. You could also be listening scribes for one another, allowing one to muse and reflect out loud while the other takes down his or her exact words as a basis for further writing.
2 Have a creative writing evening at your church fellowship or small group. You may wish to do some writing exercises together or agree to bring some writing to share with each other. Listen to each other's writing with the respect and attentiveness with which you would like to be heard. Underline parameters of confidentiality, and start and finish with prayer to mark out a space both accepting and secure.

Notes

1 Writing and the Word

1 James W. Pennebaker, *Opening Up: The Healing Power of Expressing Emotions* (London: Guilford Press, 1997).
2 Thomas W. Laqueur, *Religion and Respectability: Sunday Schools and Working Class Culture, 1780–1850* (New Haven, CT: Yale University Press, 1976).
3 Rachel G. Hackenberg, *Writing to God: 40 Days of Praying with My Pen* (Brewster, MA: Paraclete Press, 2011).
4 H. Cepero, *Journaling as Spiritual Practice: Encountering God through Attentive Writing* (Downers Grove, IL: InterVarsity Press, 2008).
5 Gillie Bolton, *The Therapeutic Potential of Creative Writing: Writing Myself* (London and Philadelphia, PA: Jessica Kingsley, 1999).

2 Journalling and getting started

1 From <www.journalkeeping.org/aboutbook.htm>, Luann Budd's website relating to her *Journal Keeping: Writing for Spiritual Growth* (Downers Grove, IL: InterVarsity Press, 2002).
2 Julia Cameron, *The Right to Write: An Invitation to the Writing Life* (New York: Jeremy P. Tarcher/Putnam, 2000).
3 Gillie Bolton, *The Therapeutic Potential of Creative Writing: Writing Myself* (London and Philadelphia, PA: Jessica Kingsley, 1999).
4 Tristine Rainer, *The New Diary: How to use a Journal for Self-guidance and Expanded Creativity* (New York: Jeremy P. Tarcher/Penguin, 1978; 2004).

3 Plans and prayers

1 Myra Schneider, *Writing My Way through Cancer* (London and New York: Jessica Kingsley, 2003).
2 Rachel G. Hackenberg, *Writing to God: 40 Days of Praying with My Pen* (Brewster, MA: Paraclete Press, 2011).

4 Writing letters

1 <ourletterstogod.tumblr.com>.
2 <www.letterstogod.net>.

5 Stories

1 Eugene Peterson, 'Living into God's Story', <www.biblicaltheology.ca/about/articles> (accessed March 2013).
2 See <www.amystoryteller.com>.

6 Dialogue

1 N. T. Wright, *The New Testament and the People of God* (London: SPCK, 1995; 2013).

7 Poetic writing 1

1 Rachel Mann's most recent collection is *Dazzling Darkness* (Glasgow: Wild Goose, 2012).
2 Gillie Bolton, *The Therapeutic Potential of Creative Writing: Writing Myself* (London: Jessica Kingsley, 1999).
3 See <www.jandean.co.uk>.
4 R. S. Thomas, 'The Absence', in *Collected Poems 1945–1990* (London: Phoenix, 1993), p. 361.
5 For more on Sue Mayfield's work, see <www.suemayfield.co.uk>.
6 See Linda's blog at <http://thelaughinghousewife.wordpress.com>.

9 Writing through loss towards healing

1 Jane Moss, *Writing in Bereavement: A Creative Handbook* (London: Jessica Kingsley, 2012).
2 Louise De Salvo, *Writing as a Way of Healing: How Telling Stories Transforms our Lives* (London: Women's Press, 1999).
3 Dorothy M. Stewart, *One Day at a Time: Meditations for Carers* (London: SPCK, 2012).
4 See Mandy's blog at <www.mandybakerjohnson.com>.
5 You can read this story at <www.john3-16.net/Michael-1.htm>.
6 For this and more of Sally's stories, go to <www.cabrinicare.wordpress.com/category/personal/>.
7 John Ortberg, *The Me I Want to be Me: Becoming God's Best Version of You* (Grand Rapids, MI: Zondervan, 2010).

10 Writing for growth

1 Russ Parker, *Healing Dreams: Their Power and Purpose in your Spiritual Life* (London: SPCK, 1993).
2 Gillie Bolton, *The Therapeutic Potential of Creative Writing: Writing Myself* (London: Jessica Kingsley, 1999).
3 Nancy Kline, *Time to Think: Listening to Ignite the Human Mind* (London: Cassell Illustrated, 1999).

11 Writing to, with and for others

1 <www.focusonthefamily.com/parenting/spiritual_growth_for_kids/ blessing-your-child/written-blessing.aspx>.
2 Andrew's blog is at <http://mildlyconfused.blogspot.co.uk>.
3 See <http://carolynhughesthehurthealer.com>.